The Complete Volleyball Handbook

Supervising Editor:
Bob Bertucci

Toshiaki Yoshida
Makoto Katsumoto
Yasumi Nakanishi

COACHES CHOICE™

ISBN: 978-1-60679-197-4
Library of Congress Control Number: 2011943221

Cover design: Bean Creek Studio
Cover photo: Courtesy of Brent Hugo and Lehigh University Athletics Department

Text photos: Courtesy of Brent Hugo and Lehigh University Athletics Department
Diagrams: Brenden Murphy
Illustrations & layout: Bean Creek Studio
Translators: Jeffrey L. King, Andrea Yough, Sandi Mather

Coaches Choice
P.O. Box 1828
Monterey, CA 93942
www.coacheschoice.com

Dedication

To parents throughout the generations, with thanks for their support,
their encouragement, the confidence they sought to instill,
and their guidance in enabling athletes to test their limits.

Acknowledgments

To properly acknowledge the people who assisted with the writing of this book requires explanation of its origin and evolution. The concept sprang from a friendship between Toshi Yoshida and me which developed while we worked with the USA Volleyball women's national program. As we discussed a wealth of volleyball issues, our conversations touched on texts and papers Toshi and other Japanese coaches had written. As I already utilized a number of Far Eastern concepts and practices in my coaching, our conversations inspired the idea of presenting such information in a basic form to a broad American audience.

Beginning with Akiko Hatakeyama, an ex-player of mine and perennial senior staff at my camps, translating the writings of Toshi and his colleagues became a summer project. I cannot thank Akiko enough for her investment of countless hours meticulously translating the Japanese writings into English. I also have to thank my good friend, colleague, and former assistant coach YiQing Weng for his efforts in continuing the translations. As a former Chinese national team player and professional player in Japan, YiQing's technical expertise added a unique perspective to the translation.

The project gradually progressed from concept to the translation from Japanese to English and finally from literal translation to, I hope, interesting reading. As we struggled to transform literal translations to American English, the rules of the game changed dramatically (e.g., introduction of the libero, allowance of the net serve, widening the service area to the whole back line, and allowance of multiple contacts on the first touch). I felt it necessary to touch on such rules in finalizing this text on volleyball. The "Americanizing" of language and additional substance infused the book with a great many more of my thoughts than originally contemplated. When I felt a particular doctrine or practice was too inflexible or narrowly applicable, I softened a statement or added an alternative drill, practice, or theory from my own experience.

To the extent the book reads well, I must thank two indispensable helpers. It is difficult to state in mere words my gratitude to my beloved wife, Tina, a volleyball expert in her own right. In addition to her infinite support, tolerance, and encouragement, Tina provided a unique perspective as a former elite player and gifted teacher of youth, junior, and collegiate players. She spent countless hours typing and acting as a sounding board for how ideas and concepts might apply to American players, coaches, and parents. I also want to thank my good friend, Dave Lockwood. By discussing issues from or about the book during our weekly workouts, I gradually piqued his interest and was able to enlist his assistance with the book, first idea by idea and then chapter by chapter. Concerned with the American reader, he ultimately rewrote the book in a more familiar and pleasing style. Just as I did, he suggested substantive additions or alternatives based on his experiences as a referee, coach, administrator, and player.

Last but certainly not least, I want to acknowledge Dr. Jim Peterson. Jim believed in, and challenged, me as a novice coach at the United States Military Academy at West Point. He encouraged me to embark on my first writings on or about athletics. In the ensuing decades, he has continued to support, collaborate on, and improve my instructional and educational writings. I treasure his insight, knowledge, humor, and, above all, friendship.

—Bob Bertucci

Contents

Preface

Following the invention of volleyball in 1895 by an American named William Morgan, it has become a sport widely enjoyed throughout the world. The FIVB (Fédération Internationale de Volleyball) has 220 member countries. Soccer, though it is called the world's sport, has 208 countries in its federation, while basketball has 213 and baseball has only 119. Thus, it is more accurate to say that volleyball is the most widely played ball sport in the world. In other words, volleyball is an excellent sport that can be enjoyed by great numbers of people all over the world.

Volleyball is played in a variety of ways and places and by a wide range of age groups. Professional leagues are found all over the world. It is also taught as a part of the physical education curriculum in schools, played by students during the lunch break and at recreational tournaments in schools. It is also played at workplaces, on beaches, and by everyone from homemakers to professional athletes. Through the years, volleyball has evolved to meet a variety of needs and is now played by a diverse body of people.

Recently, awareness of the importance of lifetime sports has been increasing. "Lifetime sports" refers to sports and activities that individuals choose to participate in throughout their lives, which are voluntarily and freely undertaken as a part of their lifestyles. Given that it is able to satisfy a wide range of needs, volleyball could thus be considered the most suitable sport for this purpose. Volleyball has the potential to enrich people's physical well-being in the 21st century.

Volleyball, however, has recently faced several difficulties, such as decreasing numbers of players and lack of spectator appeal. In order for volleyball to contribute to people's physical health and entertainment in the 21st century, a few conditions must be met in order to deal with these problems. It is first necessary that the sport be made more enjoyable for players and spectators. The addition of the "libero" has given hope to all smaller players that they are still able to play the great game of volleyball. The use of rally scoring has also contributed to a more intense game of volleyball for the players as well as a much more exciting game for the spectators. Also, coaches and those with an interest in volleyball need to introduce the appreciation and appeal of volleyball to others.

This book was written with the hope that it will help to enrich the sport of volleyball for players, teachers, and coaches alike, while helping the sport to continue to grow and develop. We hope that it will especially provide coaches, teachers, and players with a base from which to develop their creativity and energy.

Introduction

Creative Volleyball

The process of mastering the skills of a sport is actually the process of acquiring confidence through invention and practical experiences gained through practice. What is most important is for players to make use of what they learn in practice and actual matches to develop optimum technical skills and strategy. Any successes achieved by putting these into practice will help to create confidence in the skills and strategies learned. Skills and strategies personally developed through wisdom and experience become internalized and useable. Anyone who uses their own wisdom and experience to create their own skills and strategies will therefore have faith in and make full use of those skills and strategies.

This concept is particularly important for a coach. A clear difference can be found between teaching knowledge the recipients understand and knowledge the recipients can trust. It is certainly important to be familiar with a wide range of volleyball-related information; however, only taking in the information will not serve any purpose. The information must be able to be used as a base for creativity and practical implementation. Repeated successes will lead to the development of a belief in the skills, which is the path to becoming an effective player. Coaching is a long-term process as well as a creative one. Outstanding players and coaches are characterized by their high degree of creativity.

Both players and coaches who read this book have expectations that the skills and strategies presented here will be of immediate use. In response to these expectations, we have included reliable material that can be applied immediately, including keys to skill development and practice drills. As mentioned previously, the key is to use what is presented here to create something which is in line with your own individual needs.

We can't directly impart creativity and successful experiences for you. What is possible for us to do in these pages, however, is to provide an impetus for creativity and explain the underlying rationale for success in volleyball. That is our primary goal.

Scope of the Book

This book consists of seven chapters. Chapter 1 presents the characteristics of volleyball, Chapter 2 is the skills guide, Chapter 3 focuses on building the game, Chapter 4 explains the systems of play, Chapter 5 is the coaching guide, Chapter 6 addresses conditioning, and Chapter 7 is the rule guide.

In this book, we use the phrases "basic" and "advanced" to describe either the level of skills required or the degree of difficulty of the drills. Items marked basic should be mastered, as they indicate the fundamental skills of the sport. Advanced represents activities designed to achieve a higher level of skills, which will help players make use of their skills in a wider variety of situations.

We have included illustrations to supplement the technical points explained in this section in order to stimulate the creativity of the readers. These eye-catching illustrations have been computer-generated from pictures and videos, and should be more conducive to learning than plain photographs. We invite you to examine them closely; there is no telling what possibilities they will open up.

Chapter 1: The Essence of Volleyball

In order to help you gain a complete understanding of each and every element that comprises volleyball, also known as the spirit of volleyball, this chapter presents an overview of the sport's main characteristics. This information will help in building an understanding of volleyball in new players, as well as to assist coaches to break through any wall that might be standing in the way of further development.

Chapter 2: Skills Guide

This chapter mainly provides an explanation of volleyball skills. First is a description of the five most basic skills needed in a game situation. Players will enjoy playing volleyball more once they master these skills because they will be able to keep rallying for longer periods of time. The information presented is not focused solely on building skills for beginners. It also provides the opportunity for advanced players and coaches to confirm and cement their understanding of the basics.

Chapter 3: Building the Game

In order to augment the level of understanding of the game, we examine the individual skills of receive, set, and attack. These three skills make up the basic framework of offensive plays. Details on both the key points of each play and the various skills are presented in order to enhance the level of abilities in putting together offensive plays.

Chapter 4: Systems of Play

This chapter focuses on the necessary information for playing a game under the six-player system and for understanding the mechanics of the playing system. We look at the need for a team to have an organized pattern of plays. This methodical system is required to ensure that the abilities of each player on the court are used to the fullest. It is sure to be very effective in creating a cohesive team.

Chapter 5: Coaching Guide

The main theme of this book is the importance of being creative in volleyball, and this chapter is what we consider its most distinctive feature. In addition to presenting philosophies about the skills and strategies necessary to coaching, we provide a variety of aids to help create skills and strategies, inventive drills, and practice methods. These aids are sure to be of use for coaches.

Chapter 6: Conditioning for Volleyball

Every sport played competitively requires some degree of conditioning to ensure a competitive advantage. This chapter will address some conditioning principles and methods that will allow the athlete or coach a simple well-balanced approach.

Chapter 7: Rules Guide

Volleyball is a sport that people have found a variety of ways to play. This book focuses on the six-player system and explains the current rules of that system and other necessary information in an easy-to-understand format.

—Toshiaki Yoshida

1

The Essence of Volleyball

Playing and coaching volleyball require an understanding of the core elements and the essence of the sport. This chapter will discuss the characteristics which distinguish volleyball to increase the reader's understanding of the game.

It is essential for players and coaches to understand the components of volleyball technique and strategy (its structural characteristics), as well as how to take pleasure in the game (its functional characteristics). Knowledge of the characteristics of volleyball strengthen appreciation of its spirit and facilitate the improvement of technique and strategy in a logical, effective manner. Familiarity with volleyball's particular characteristics is the first step toward its mastery.

The Ultimate Team Sport

Under its rules, volleyball cannot be played alone. The rules prohibit one player from handling or directing the ball on consecutive plays. In other words, one outstanding player cannot dominate the game by performing all elements of a play (i.e., serving, serve receive, passing, setting, spiking, and/or blocking). Volleyball requires all team members to coordinate and cooperate to achieve optimal results. For this reason, volleyball is often called the ultimate team sport.

Figure 1-1. Volleyball is often called the ultimate team sport.

It is important for each player to become proficient in the fundamental skills (passing, receiving, attacking, serving, setting, blocking, etc.). To improve overall team performance, each player must also develop a thorough understanding of the choreography and coordination that define plays and formations. No matter how skilled each team member is, if the six players on the court cannot coordinate their efforts and play as a unit, they will fail, permitting the ball to fall between them, neglecting to assist with a key block, failing to lure a blocker with a fake, incorrectly hitting a ball following a failure to communicate the play or set, and/or interfering with each other's efforts to play the ball. A strong team cannot be built without coordination among the players. This is why a team with highly skilled individual players but lacking psychological and technical cohesion often will not achieve the success of a team with less skilled players who work well together. Thus, a superior team is the culmination of individual skill integrated into teamwork. The rapid pace of action on a volleyball court makes this fact is even truer for the sport than for most other team sports. The various aspects of playing this game intertwine to create a sport that is fascinating at many levels.

Simple: No Special Equipment Is Needed

Volleyball, baseball, soccer, and golf all involve hitting a ball in some manner. Among these sports, volleyball is one of the few which can be played with minimal or no additional apparatus. Unlike sports that require fancy or expensive equipment, people easily and quickly can organize an enjoyable game of volleyball. Furthermore, the game can be played nearly everywhere. For example, two players can pepper (pass or set the ball back and forth), three players can practice serving and receiving, and four players complete a doubles game. Volleyball can be played by anyone, anywhere at any time. The sport's popularity has spread around the world; membership in the FIVB has exploded to 220 countries.

Figure 1-2. Volleyball is one of the few ball sports that can be played with minimal or no additional apparatus.

When volleyball was invented, the ball was a rubber inner tube covered with leather or linen. In size, it was similar to modern volleyballs, but it was up to one-and-a-half times heavier than the modern ball. Over time, improvements were made in, and standards were set for, the weight and pliability of the ball, reducing the impact on players' hands and arms. These improvements helped volleyball become a sport that people of all ages could play and enjoy. Indeed, the USA Volleyball National Championships include adult age group categories in five-year increments, including an age group with a minimum age of 75. Corresponding Junior Olympic age group categories keep getting younger and doubled not long ago by reducing each category increment from two years to one year. Popular variations of volleyball continue to develop around the world, including soft volleyball, U-volleyball (with maximum height restrictions), wallyball (played on racquetball courts), grass volleyball, mud volleyball, beach volleyball, and nine-man volleyball (a resurgence of the original game as preserved in remote Chinese villages and spreading in the United States and elsewhere).

Hitting: The Ball Cannot Be Held

William P. Morgan invented volleyball in 1895 for patrons of the YMCA in Holyoke, Massachusetts. He planned for the sport to be a "less vigorous" alternative to the then recently invented sport of basketball down the road at the Springfield, Massachusetts YMCA. Mr. Morgan named his sport "mintonette." Gradually, people began to refer to the sport as "volleyball" based on its essential activity of passing the ball back and forth without letting it touch the floor.

Since the ball must be volleyed, holding (stopping its motion) is not allowed. Holding the ball can result in a fault or loss of the rally with a point awarded to the (opposing) team, which did not hold the ball. This prohibition against holding the ball is what makes ball control difficult and fundamental in volleyball. In sports where the ball can be held, if a player's physical position and setup are a little off for a play, the problem can be corrected by stopping or holding onto the ball and then completing the pass. In volleyball, however, this is not possible. Attempting a play without being in good or proper position often results in a bad pass or handling the ball in a manner unacceptable under the sport's rules. It is, therefore, critical to get set in the ready position before touching the ball, with proper hand and foot positions and limbs flexed. In volleyball, preparation is everything.

Figure 1-3. The prohibition against holding the ball is what makes ball control difficult and fundamental in volleyball.

Correcting another player's imperfect handling of the ball is another key element of the game. Ball control is difficult under any circumstances. When faced with an opponent's fierce attack or jump serve, successful passing of the ball to a desired location occurs less than half the time. It is best for players to assume from the start that the ball will not always go where they want it and to accept this result as a normal part of the game. This frequency of imperfect handling is what makes mending, or continuing the play after an inaccurate contact, so important. The ball shoots back and forth unpredictably, so even when a teammate has the ball, a player should anticipate the need to improve subsequent contacts.

Volleying: The Ball Should Not Touch the Floor

When the ball contacts one team's side of the volleyball court, the opposing team earns a point; thus, the court surface in volleyball can be compared to the goal box in soccer. In volleyball, the opposing teams use various methods of attack as each competes to make the ball contact the other team's court surface or contact an opposing player before going out-of-bounds. Top-level teams in particular develop and practice attacks designed to trick the opponent into letting the ball fall to the court. Such game tactics include combination attacks, quick attacks, and back row attacks. For these reasons, it is important to have a strong offense, be able to attack and score points, and present a strong defense to prevent the opponent from scoring points. How well a team plans and executes receiving formations or blocks counter-attacks also has a direct impact on scoring points. Finally, a team's errors and faults (handling errors, touching the net, etc.) directly result in points for the opposition. These kinds of points often turn the tide of the game. To some degree, volleyball could be described as an error-driven sport, which is why it is so important to minimize the number of mistakes. Unforced errors include touching the net, penetration faults, positional faults, lifted balls, double contacts, hitting out-of-bounds, and four-hit faults. These faults are probably the worst kind of errors to make because they are avoidable and generally not caused by the skill of an opposing team. Dedicated players and committed teams make the fewest mistakes (unforced errors) and maximize their potential.

Figure 1-4. The court surface in volleyball can be compared to the goal box in soccer.

Clearly, a strong team balances an aggressive offense with a skilled defense and commits few errors. The continuous switching between offense and defense defines volleyball and its rhythm.

The Court Is Divided by a Net

A net evenly divides each volleyball court, and the sport's rules prohibit physical contact between opposing players. Other net sports include badminton, tennis, and table tennis, but the rules differ for each of them, and they especially differ from volleyball.

Figure 1-5. A net evenly divides each volleyball court.

As mentioned, a feature of all sports in which a net divides the playing surface is that there is no direct physical contact between opposing teams or players. This feature means a player can concentrate on making a play without interference when the ball comes to his side. Consequently, a team's proficiency or skill inevitably determines who wins or loses a game. The majority of practice time, therefore, should be devoted to improving ball control techniques While most net sports are played with one or two people to a side so that individual practice and skills directly influence the outcome of a competition, six players compete on each side in (indoor) volleyball, making coordination with teammates as important as individual skills. Although opposing players cannot interfere with play on the other team's half of the volleyball court, poor coordination with or awareness of teammates often will cause confusion and errors. Although lack of interference from opponents characterizes most net sports, volleyball players must still be careful about unintentional interference with teammates. On this point, volleyball is unique.

Serving

Each rally in volleyball begins with a serve. The first play of the serving team is, of course, the serve, and the first play of the non-serving team is receiving the serve. A strong, accurate, and/or deceptive serve and an effective or consistent serve receive are critical to a team's success and often decide the outcome of a game.

Figure 1-6. Each rally in volleyball begins with a serve.

From the moment a ball is contacted for service until the referee blows the whistle to stop play, a player's attention should not waver even for an instant. From the end of the rally until the next serve, there is a bit of down time, when a player may relax slightly and contemplate issues such as the reasons for mistakes, the score, refocusing, and so on. The mental and emotional states of players particularly impact volleyball matches. This impact is greatest when the team is on a high, but the ability to maintain composure and focus after an error is equally important. Probably the best mental approach during the time between rallies is to regroup mentally, (re)focus on how to improve personal play during the next rally, and identify what elements from the previous play (or earlier plays) succeeded and failed.

The mental state of a volleyball player from the end of a rally to the next serve or serve receive directly impacts the quality of physical performance and how well he applies the skills and techniques taught in practice. Because of the importance of the outcome of serves and receiving serves in determining the outcome of a game, a player's attitude preceding a play is very important.

System-Oriented:
High Concentration of Players on the Court

Compared to other ball sports such as soccer and basketball, volleyball has a dense concentration of players for its playing space. Soccer has one person per 490.9 square meters (120 x 90 m / 22 people) and basketball one person per 42 square meters, while volleyball has one person per 13.5 square meters (9 x 18 m / 12 people). In volleyball, three people occupy the space accorded one player in basketball. Because of this density, volleyball players sometimes collide or interfere with each other. Consequently, the ball sometimes drops between two players who fail to communicate or who are playing out of (proper) position.

Figure 1-7. Volleyball has a dense concentration of players for its playing space.

The density or close proximity of players on a volleyball court, in turn, means that player movements must be systematic. The interrelationships between teammates will vary with the rotation, game situation, and actions of the opposing team. Such interrelationships (including alternatives when one strategy does not succeed) should be studied, anticipated, practiced, and well established before a match begins. Such variables include the individual lateral relationships among the three front row players and among the three back row players, the front/back relationships between these players, and the overall group. Other relationship variables include planning how to receive, dilute, defeat, or deflect an opposing team's offensive attack, deciding which player will take what action in a combination attack, and other nuances of offense and defense. The organization of team members, coordination of their movements, and how they should interact on the court must be clearly decided and established before competition.

Aggressive: Offense and Defense Are Not Equal

Volleyball resembles soccer in that both sports involve an adversary team seeking to mount an offensive attack, but it differs dramatically in scoring frequency. If a strong offense is mounted in volleyball, the opposing team often cannot defend successfully against the attack. In a battle between offensive power and defensive power, the winner in volleyball most often will be offensive power.

Figure 1-8. In a battle between offensive power and defensive power, the winner in volleyball most often will be offensive power.

For example, statistics for international level volleyball competitions indicate that the serving team will win the rally (and score a point) more than 70 percent of the time. In the battle between offense and defense, therefore, the breakdown is not 50/50, but rather 70/30 or greater in favor of the offense. This serving (offense) advantage also exists in lower level and even novice competitions. Of course, when both teams lack offensive power, the stronger defensive team is sure to win. Nonetheless, when one team possesses distinctively stronger servers or attackers, the game will often become one-sided in favor of that team. A team that lacks the offensive capability to earn a side-out and regain the serve inevitably will get blown out. The soccer strategy of "Score one goal, and the rest is just defense" will not work in volleyball. Volleyball requires players to be on offense until the last point is awarded. Players must compete aggressively and offensively every moment until the bitter end of a match. The saying that the best defense is a good offense really does apply in volleyball.

Rotations

Players rotate in traditional six-person volleyball. When a team earns a side-out, its players rotate clockwise one position. This is a rotation. In volleyball lingo, it is common to identify the position or pre-service location of the player in the serving position (back right as facing the net) as position 1. The player who next will rotate to the service position (front right) is designated as position 2; next (middle front) is position 3; next (left front) is position 4; next (left back) is position 5; and finally (middle back) is position 6. These six positions are those through which a player rotates.

At the moment of service, players may be anywhere on the court if they are not overlapped with adjacent teammates. For example, the player in position 1 (back right) cannot be closer to the net than the player in position 2 (front right). Correspondingly, the position 2 player cannot be closer to the end (back) line than the position 1 player. The same restrictions apply with the adjacent side players. If either referee notices a significant overlap (more than a gratuitous foot or so) at the moment the ball is contacted for service, the referee will whistle the violation and award a point to the opposing team. Notwithstanding, within the positional rules, many complicated and deceptive serve receive positional arrangements are available/legal.

Once the serve has been contacted for service, players may move anywhere on the court with respect to teammates. The only restrictions pertain to certain offensive actions back row players may not take on or in front of the line drawn on their side of the court parallel to, and three meters away from, the center line (line under the net dividing the court in two equal halves). Since most players must play both front row and back row, the ideal player possesses all-around (offensive and defensive) skills. Depending on the course of a game, it can be beneficial to have players who are highly skilled in one area (specialized), such as blocking or passing, in addition to the multi-dimensional players on the roster. Part of the art of coaching involves blending the specialized players with the all-round players so the weaknesses of the specialists are hidden or minimized and their strengths maximized (if they play front and back rows). Another aspect of the art focuses on timely insertion (substitution) of specialized players for the same reasons. Such blending helps to maximize a team's performance on the court.

With six players rotating around the court, coaches can design six different sets of offensive and defensive positional patterns. Each rotation's pattern will offer different strengths and weaknesses, but each rotation must be designed to avoid an extreme deficiency in either offense or defense. It is the coach's responsibility to identify the skills, strengths, weaknesses, character, and potential of each player on the roster and then develop lineups and alternatives to maximize team performance and address specific game situations as they arise.

What Is Fun About Volleyball?

Volleyball could be described as a physical contest in which two teams face each other through a raised net as though gazing into a mirror across a net with constant transition between offense and defense, utilizing the skills of serving, passing, setting, spiking, blocking, and receiving. Novice players often enjoy practicing specific or fundamental skills of the sport more than playing a game frequently interrupted by their lack of skill. Players have the opportunity to contact the ball far more often during a practice of fundamentals than during a game, resulting in the opportunity for, and pleasure of, improvement. In parallel fashion, playing a game without basic skills and/or teammates reluctant to pass the ball to an unskilled player is no fun at all. As a player's volleyball skills improve, a coach will engage the player in more sophisticated drills, including game variations with an increasing number of teammates or even in an actual game.

Figure 1-9. It is important for coaches to encourage play and practice that keep the game fun.

One study polled university volleyball players about why volleyball is fun. Among other reasons, university athletes explained that they enjoyed the following aspects of volleyball:

- The joy of succeeding as a team rather than as unassociated individuals
- The intensity and passion of a match against a fierce rival
- Those moments when everything "clicks" and the level of individual or team play rises beyond expectation
- Times when play, practice, or shared time off the court is lighthearted and fun
- Being praised for improvement or doing something well
- The moment when a player finally understands a skill, strategy, or nuance of the game
- The satisfaction of pounding a good spike

Responses on a questionnaire completed by junior high school student athletes were similar. Volleyball's unique balance of a need for true teamwork with the opportunity to improve and shine as an individual player, the chance to play the game at any age, and the unusually strong requirement for sportsmanship imbued in its rules make it fun to learn and play. It is important for coaches and other persons in leadership positions to encourage play and practice that keep the game fun even for scholarship athletes or youth players aspiring to a scholarship. In most situations, a coach or organizer should strive to create a positive, relaxed environment with practices and matches that satisfy the needs of the greatest number of players possible, setting up many different kinds (and levels) of games and drills so everyone can share in the fun.

As seen in Figure 1-10, sports can be divided into team-oriented, individual-oriented, natural, and artificial categories. Volleyball is a very human sport, and, at its highest levels, inspires awe with the power and speed of spikes and jump serves. It elicits gasps at the gymnastic digs that prevent such hits from striking the floor. Although it is a team sport, many plays require individual skill. Volleyball's international popularity continues to rise, behind only soccer and ahead of basketball, baseball, hockey, and other sports. Volleyball is a great game, which can be played competitively or casually. This book will endeavor to increase the reader's enjoyment of the game by explaining some of volleyball's finer points and by providing information which should facilitate growth and improvement as a coach or player.

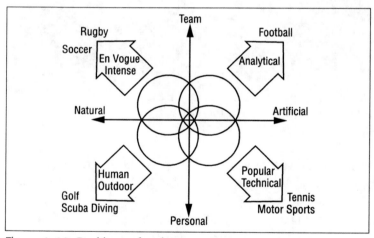

Figure 1-10. Positions of various sports

2

Skills Guide

This chapter introduces and describes the five basic skills that compose the game of volleyball, different ways of receiving and attacking, and practice points and drills for mastering skills.

The Overhand Pass

Rule changes over the past decade have made overhand passing the most important skill in volleyball. Overhand passing is a skill with broad application, used in a game to receive and set the ball, as well as a means of offense by shooting the ball over the net to an open or undefended location on the far court. Beginners can maintain a series of consecutive overhand passes longer than a series of consecutive underhand passes. Mastering overhand passing is key to developing solid ball control. As overhand passing has become the primary technique for controlling the ball, coaches should dedicate generous time to its practice.

Fundamentals of Overhand Passing

The following numbers correspond to the numbers in Figure 2-1:
1. Flex the ankles and knees, and move swiftly to the spot where the ball is falling.
2. Keep the elbows and wrists loose, lift the arms, and look at the ball through the triangular window created by thumbs and index fingers.

3. Coordinate movements to meet the ball as it falls, by bending the ankles, knees, and elbows, so the ball comes to the player rather than the player reaching for the ball.

4. "Catch" or control the ball for an instant. The rule change some years ago permitting multiple contacts when receiving a first (spiked or served) ball using finger action created a much more liberal interpretation of legal first contacts. Many first contacts, which would have been deemed a carry or lift, are now legal. Nonetheless, avoid having the ball come to a stop when receiving a first ball for an overhand pass, as lifts technically remain illegal.

5. Push the ball outward, using the spring from elbows and knees, and step slightly forward for the follow-through while keeping the eyes on the ball.

Figure 2-1. Fundamentals of overhand passing

Tips on Overhand Passing (Figure 2-2)

When practicing overhand passes, it is important for players to remember correct hand position, the position for receiving the ball, and the coordinated technique or process for receiving the ball (how to use the wrists, elbows, and knees in unison). As with any

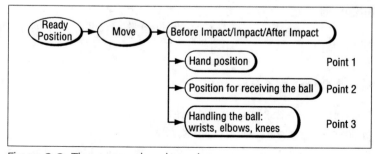

Figure 2-2. Tips on overhand passing

skill, sufficient practice should make these techniques automatic so that it is no longer necessary to think about them.

• Point 1: Hand position—Make an opening between both hands (Figure 2-3)

The player should put both arms in the air with the elbows bent, as shown in Figure 2-3. The fingers of both hands should be open in a mirror image, as if to wrap them around the near half of the ball. The player should be particularly aware of the position of thumbs, index fingers, and small fingers, forming a loose triangle with the thumbs and index fingers. To confirm proper technique in practice, it can be helpful to have the player catch the ball from time to time and examine finger placement on the ball.

Figure 2-3. Hand position

• Point 2: Position for receiving the ball (Figure 2-4)

The player should receive the ball in the space above the top center of the forehead. He should look up at the ball, receiving it whenever possible near the forehead. A good test to confirm proper position in practice is to spread or remove the hands from

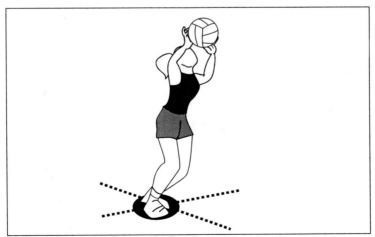

Figure 2-4. Position for receiving the ball

time to time so the incoming ball strikes the forehead. The ball should hit the middle forehead and rebound true, as with a soccer header.

• Point 3: Handling the ball (Figure 2-5)

The basic technique for handling the ball requires flexing the wrists, elbows, and knees to catch the ball momentarily, and then extending them to release or propel the ball. First, the player should relax the hip, knee, and ankle joints so they are loose and flexible and ready to move in any direction. Then, he should move swiftly to the spot where the ball will fall, and with bent elbows, knees, and ankles, move to meet the ball. Ankles and knees must be bent and ready before the ball ever touches the hands; they should be at their deepest bend at the instant the ball first contacts the hands. Using the spring created by this flex or compression, the player should extend the body (straightening knees and ankles), releasing the force in elbow, knee, and ankle joints simultaneously to push the ball in the desired direction.

Figure 2-5. Handling the ball

Soft Passes—Free Balls

Overhand passing a softly falling ball requires a technique almost identical to the method of handling the ball explained in the previous section. Body actions should be coordinated to meet the ball, bending elbows, and catching the ball for an instant. It is probably best to bend wrists backward a modest amount because the softly falling ball has less rebound energy than a hard hit spike or serve. As the ball enters the hands, the player should loosen the elbows and wrists to receive it, as if the ball is being suctioned into the hands. Immediately thereafter, the spring contained in the flexed elbows and wrists should be released to propel the ball away.

Hard Passes—Receiving Serves and Attacks

When anticipating a hard hit serve or attack, the tension in the hands, elbows, wrists, and corresponding joints should be strengthened to avoid having the hard hit ball power through. Greater strength is required to control a hard hit ball than a softly falling ball. Failure to use sufficient strength or control in receiving a driven ball will result in an inaccurate (shanked or off-target) or, worse, illegal (lifted or carried) pass.

Practice Drills

The basic drills for practicing passes involve two persons. The drills should be performed with variations in distance and height. As players or teams develop skills and confidence, it is optimum to practice drills involving game situations (e.g., pass, set, spike, and sometimes block).

Basic—Sitting Pass (Figure 2-6)

The players should sit on the ground and practice passing. Concentrate first on the proper technique for use of elbows and wrists. Concentrate second on accurate passing. In this drill, an accurate pass would descend on the central upper forehead of the opposite (sitting) player. This drill addresses fundamental passing techniques, especially with respect to softly descending (free) balls.

Figure 2-6. Sitting pass (basic)

Basic—Two-Person Continuous Pass

The goal is 30 to 50 continuous passes. More than 100 consecutive and continuous passes would be advanced. This drill can be practiced sitting or standing. If standing, a player must also concentrate on proper technique for moving to the ball and flexion of the ankles and knees. A helpful variation of this drill has one player passing the ball slightly away from the other player so she will be reminded of the need to move to the ball as it descends to optimize good position when receiving.

Advanced—Overhand Pass for Hard Hits (Figure 2-7)

Have one player hit the ball to a partner. The partner then should pass the ball to a certain point or back to the serving/hitting player. If practiced with a net, this drill is an elementary form of a game situation practice. Adding elements to the drill such as a serve, pass to a setter, set to a hitter, spike, continuous play, and other variables increases the completeness of the game situation drill.

Figure 2-7. Overhand pass for hard hits (advanced)

Advanced—Overhead Back Pass (Figure 2-8)

One player should toss the ball directly overhead, move (if necessary) to where the ball is descending, and then back set or pass the ball to a partner who should receive

Figure 2-8. Overhead back pass (advanced)

it facing the ball. The partner then should pass the ball straight up, turn 180 degrees, and then back set the ball to the original passer (who has turned around). Both passers should endeavor to maintain the now-established pattern without losing control. The goals are to perform a good (straight) overhead toss, move quickly to the position where the ball will fall (ideally, little or no distance away), complete a half revolution, and perform an accurate back pass or set. The back pass is performed by receiving the ball in the proper location (with space above the forehead), and then extending both hands back over the head. This drill emphasizes technique, concentration, and control.

The Underhand (Forearm) Pass

The underhand pass, like the overhand pass, is a primary and critically fundamental volleyball skill that players must master. It is the technique used to pass balls below the hips and balls hit with so much power it would be impossible to utilize the overhead pass without (illegally) holding or carrying the ball. Since this pass is a relatively simple action (hitting the ball with the arms), it is the pass used by many beginners. However, even a small miscalculation in technique can send the ball flying in the wrong direction. Accordingly, proper technique is essential for control.

The overhead pass involves forming a basket with the hands and letting the compressed energy of bent elbows, knees, ankles, and sometimes wrists fling the ball away. In comparison, the underhand pass utilizes a flattened "V" surface (often referred to as the platform) formed by the forearms, the compressed energy of flexed knees and ankles, and the rebound energy of the driven ball off the platform to propel and direct the ball.

Balls stay in contact with an underhand passer for a shorter time than with an overhand passer. In addition, an underhand passing platform exerts controlling energy on only two sides of the ball (from the near-parallel arms), while the overhand passer exerts controlling energy on four sides. By the laws of physics, the overhand pass will tend to control the ball more accurately than an underhand pass.

Fundamentals of Underhand Passing

The following numbers correspond to the numbers in Figure 2-9:
1. Relax the shoulders, bend the knees slightly, and, in this relaxed condition, use the compressed legs, ankles, and knees to rise and meet the ball. In meeting the ball, there is a slight forward movement of the body. It is critical not to be flat-footed, but, rather, poised, on the front of the feet prepared to adjust to floating, curving, or diving balls. Remember that knees and ankles are bent—coiled like a spring to absorb some of the force of a hard driven ball and containing compressed force, as needed, to direct a ball in the desired direction and/or propel a soft-driven ball.

2. Prepare to receive the ball by moving a step or two behind where the ball is expected to fall. Clasp the hands in front so that the forearm surfaces create a flat platform (a wide V), and with arms extended. The downward angle of the extended arms will vary with the distance needed to pass the ball and whether the setter/play requires a soft (high arc) or fast/tight (low parabola) pass. The default is always a high pass so the setter can adjust to problems in the pass or developing play.

3. Line up with the ball as it falls, and take a step forward to meet it.

4. The ball should hit near the heel of the hand, in the wrist and lower forearm area. Note that the ball should strike the widest part of the lower forearm. Too tight or narrow a V will cause the ball to strike the ulna (long narrow) bones running along the inside part of the arm—a smaller, less controlled platform, and a harder surface (than the wide part of the lower forearm), creating a more variable rebound.

5. Do not carry the ball with arm and shoulder strength alone; be conscious of using the whole body, especially the lower half.

Figure 2-9. Fundamentals of underhand passing

Tips on Underhand Passing (Figure 2-10)

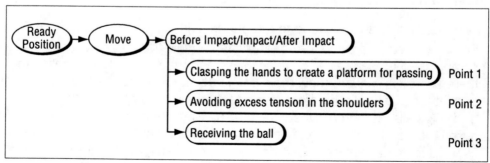

Figure 2-10. Tips on underhand passing

• Point 1: Clasping the hands to create a platform for passing (Figure 2-11)

If a proper platform with the forearms is not created to receive the ball, control of the pass/ball likely will be poor. The player should master the method of clasping hands by either crossing the fingers and putting the heels of the hands together with the thumbs parallel or interlocking the fingers. Both methods of clasping create a flat surface, where the ball will hit on the forearms. Too tight or long of a grip limits arm movement, so the hands should come together and interlock only for the moment before and at contact with the ball.

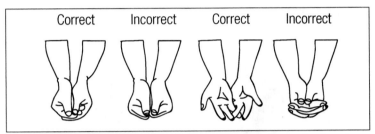

Figure 2-11. Clasping the hands to create a platform for passing

• Point 2: Avoiding excess tension in the shoulders (Figure 2-12)

After creating a good platform with the arms, the next element of technique for the underhand pass is adjusting to the speed and power of the incoming ball in part through musculature tension. The extended arms should resemble a flat board with a center groove. Overuse of the shoulders should be avoided. Players who focus too much on their platform often use too much shoulder strength when passing the ball. Too much tension in the shoulders makes it difficult to adjust the platform for a hard, soft, or intermediately driven ball. For example, more tension causes the platform surface to become hard and unyielding, which undermines the ability to perform soft or gently looping passes. Players must remember to relax the shoulders.

Figure 2-12. Avoiding excess tension in the shoulders

• Point 3: Receiving the ball (Figure 2-13)

For any type of pass, and particularly for underhand passes, it is ideal to receive the ball directly in front of the body. As the ball is rarely (and certainly not intentionally) hit directly at a player, this ideal usually necessitates the receiver/passer moving to (and behind) the point where a hit or served ball will land. Some players shift their bodies slightly to the right or left when contacting the ball (one foot slightly in front of the other), based on comfort and balance. As demonstrated in Figure 2-13, it is important not to draw up too tightly, but rather contact the ball while keeping space along the trunk below the arms. If the body is pulled in too tightly, it is difficult to control the rebound of the passed ball.

Figure 2-13. Receiving the ball

Lower-body movement is less obvious, but is still an important element of a well-controlled pass. Imagine executing a soft underhand pass to a partner. When making a soft pass, it is necessary to use the hands in coordination with the whole body, sending the ball off at slow speed with the coordinated movement. The lower-body movement used here is the foundation of underhand passing.

Basic Body Movement

Place three or more players in each of two lines with the front player in each line facing the first person in the opposite line. Make sure the second person in each line gives the player in front space in which to back up two or three steps. Have the first player in one line toss a ball to the first person in the other line. The receiving player should back up one to three steps, and then *only* using the energy or force of forward movement (no swinging arms or rising up), walk or glide forward with the arm platform outstretched and pass the ball accurately to the front of the opposite line. The passer then should run to the end of the opposite line. The first person in the other (receiving) line should back up a step or three and then move forward through the ball to pass it back. Players should aspire to control the ball so that all drill participants move through the ball at least 10 times consecutively.

Practice Drills

Basic—Underhand Ball Receiving (Figure 2-14)

This drill practices receiving the ball in a relaxed stance. Holding the hands and shoulders with even a little force or tension in them inhibits a controlled reception and rebound (pass). The players should work to develop a sense of bringing the ball to rest gently.

Figure 2-14. Underhand ball receiving (basic)

Basic—One-Arm Vertical Pass (Figure 2-15)

This drill attempts to reinforce contacting the ball with the correct part of the arm. Balancing a ball on the wrist and forearm, the player should lift the ball with one arm. Players should practice until able to perform 10 or more consecutive repetitions. After

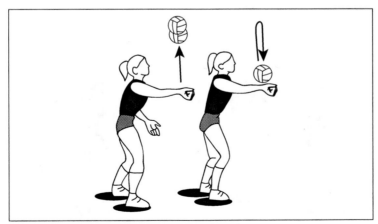

Figure 2-15. One-arm vertical pass (basic)

mastering this skill with one arm, players should switch to the other arm. Finally, practice the drill alternating between arms. An advanced variation of this drill is to practice bouncing a ball on the lower forearm and wrist of one arm until it is possible to control the bounce 10 or more times consecutively. As before, have the players switch to the other arm and then to alternating arms.

Advanced—Bound-Arm Pass (Figure 2-16)

This drill focuses on passing the ball, using lower body action. The person performing the drill stands with hands clasped in the underhand pass position while the arms are tied to hold them near the body. This prevents passing with only the arms, making it imperative to utilize lower-body motion to move the ball. The player should use the knees and work to develop a sense of transporting the ball upward by lifting or rising with the lower body.

Figure 2-16. Bound-arm pass (advanced)

Advanced—Ballhandling Pass (Figure 2-17)

Figure 2-17. Ballhandling pass (advanced)

This drill develops a sense for gently stopping the ball and sending it back to a partner. The person tossing the ball should stand three to four meters away from the receiver. In the underhand pass position, the receiver should use the arms, shoulders, and knees to "stop" or catch the ball on the lower forearm and wrist. The receiver then passes or lifts the ball back to the ball tosser, who should endeavor to receive or stop the ball in mirror fashion before passing it back. The player should work to develop a sense of using the entire body to transport the ball rather than only the arms. As control, skill, and confidence grow, the distance between partners can be increased.

The Attack

The attack is the technique used to return a ball to an opponent's court. The minimum objective is to get the ball over the net into the opponent's court. The higher goal is to attack the ball in a manner the opposition cannot return.

Fundamentals of Attacks

The following numbers correspond to the numbers in Figure 2-18:

1. Anticipate where the set ball will come down. Take two steps forward. Note: It is common and often advisable for an attacker to pull off (take several steps away from) the net after the ball has been passed to the setter so there is space to complete a full approach.

2. Time the approach (movement toward the net and set ball) to meet the ball, taking a large third step or hop to land on the back portion of both heels while swinging the arms back. The transition from one-foot steps to the two-foot landing, landing on the heels, and swinging the arms back are ways an attacker partially transfers the energy of moving forward into upward energy.

Figure 2-18. Fundamentals of attacks

3. When both feet are solidly planted after the third step or hop and the forward motion naturally causes the attacker to move from the heel to the front portion of the feet, jump into the air while swinging the arms up and forward from behind.
4. Stretch the non-hitting arm up and out as if pointing at the ball, and draw or cock the hitting arm back to hit, thrusting out the chest, with the elbow kept high. Get set with the hitting right hand near the ear and the hitting shoulder pulled back.
5. Allow the body to turn in the air as the non-hitting arm lowers, and at the same time, begin to extend the hitting arm.
6. Straighten the elbow of the hitting arm, and hit the ball while snapping the wrist. Visually focus on the ball until it lands.

Note that a proper approach and jump will have the attacker hitting the ball slightly in front of the vertical body extension. Hitting from behind a ball maximizes an attacker's ability to hit down and opens the opponent's entire court to peripheral view and attack. Conversely, hitting from under the ball (a common mistake) reduces control, power, the ability to hit down, and an attacker's view of the opposing court.

Tips on Attacks (Figure 2-19)

Attacking tips broadly divide into three categories: hitting at the maximum height, hitting the ball where intended, and using power or deception to overcome a block or defense. To put these tips into practice requires mastering proper techniques for arm swing, hitting the ball, and timing.

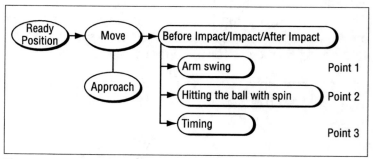

Figure 2-19. Tips on attacks

• Point 1: Arm swing (Figure 2-20)

Executing proper arm swing is vital to hitting the ball at the maximum possible height. Correct technique also reduces the possibility of injury. Conversely, improper technique (such as letting the non-hitting shoulder drop or hitting from under the set rather than from behind) reduces power and control while increasing the probability of injury.

As previously described, an attacker raises the non-hitting arm and almost points at the ball while drawing the attacking arm back, momentarily cocked behind or beside the ear. Pulling back the hitting right shoulder at this point increases the power or force applied when the ball is hit. The swing should follow through the place where the (non-hitting) elbow had been held high. In an attack, the hitting hand should travel from the ear, to the area beside and behind the head, and then forward and down. After hitting the ball (ideally at maximum height) in the area above and in front of the forehead, the arm path will naturally continue and end by the thigh.

Figure 2-20. Arm swing

• Point 2: Hitting the ball with spin (Figure 2-21)

Placement of an attacker's hand on the ball has the greatest effect on where the ball will land in the opposite court. For ideal contact with the ball, a hitter should line up the knuckle at the base of the middle finger (hitting hand) with the center of the ball. Upon contact with the ball, it is important to snap the wrist. This snap gives the ball forward (downward) spin. Balls accelerate or curve in the direction of their spin, so a forward spinning ball (attack or serve) will tend to curve or dive down quickly. Contact a set ball at the peak (highest point) of the jump, again making sure to hit the ball in front rather than from underneath. Pulling the chin in while hitting the ball makes it easier to snap the wrist.

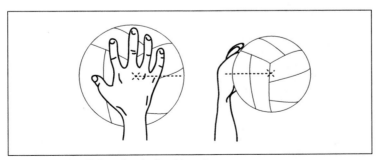

Figure 2-21. Hitting the ball with spin

• Point 3: Timing

To attack with consistent success, all of the steps involved must be executed smoothly, from the approach to where the set ball will come down, to the takeoff (the jump), the hit itself, and the landing. It is necessary to practice attacking techniques repeatedly to develop proper timing at two key junctures—the beginning of the approach and the point when an attacker is about to hit the ball with the arms up in the air. Approach speed, jumping ability, arm length, height, and wrist snap vary with the individual. Correspondingly, the timing of a player's optimal hit will vary, emphasizing the need for individual practice.

Practice Drills

Basic—Mastering Timing

- When introducing or explaining the timing of an approach, start simple with a one- or two-step approach. Have one player toss the ball (in the form of a moderately high set) from a little less than two meters away (two antenna lengths), and have the attacker start the (one- or two-step) approach when the ball is at its peak. Repeat this basic approach until the attacker is comfortable and has developed proper timing.
- Have a player practice jumping but intentionally miss the ball. If the player is maximizing his jump in coordination with proper timing and position, he should eventually be able to hit the ball with the head near the brow or hairline.

Basic—Finding the Proper Hitting Point

- Form pairs. Have one player toss or loop the ball toward the head of a partner. The partner should intentionally miss the ball, hitting it with a forward (gentle) snap of the head instead.

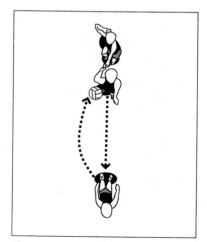

Figure 2-22. Finding the proper hitting point (in pairs)

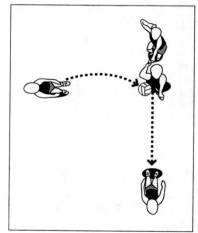

Figure 2-23. Finding the proper hitting point (in groups of three)

- Form pairs. Have one player toss the ball toward the head of a partner. The receiving player should rise without jumping and hit or spike the ball, focusing on snapping the wrist (Figure 2-22).
- Form groups of three. Have one player toss the ball from a new angle to either of the partners. The receiving partner should turn and hit the ball toward the third player (Figure 2-23).
- Repeat the previous drill, this time with the hitter including a moderate jump.

The Serve

The serve starts the game and, indeed, begins each rally. As the first offensive action of every rally, mastering the serve is crucial to team success. An effective serve defeats, disrupts, or at least challenges an opponent's serve receive, undermining the opponent's ability to counter-attack.

Furthermore, the serve is the only action in volleyball by which a single player can score a point without a teammate ever touching the ball. In junior or youth competitions, an effective serve has an especially significant impact on match outcome. Players should practice serves until they can place them with consistency, confidence, precision, and velocity.

Fundamentals of Basic Serves

The following numbers correspond to the numbers in Figure 2-24:

1. Decide from what point behind the court's end line to serve.

Figure 2-24. Fundamentals of basic serves

2. Cupping the ball in the non-serving hand, the server should toss the ball straight up, not wavering in any direction, in a manner similar to the toss for serve of a tennis ball. In fact, if a novice player has difficulty tossing the ball straight up consistently, she might practice tossing with a tennis ball, develop consistency, and then advance to a volleyball.

3. It is extremely important to ensure that the ball is tossed slightly in front of the body plane and not over the head. Frontal contact provides the developing server with a greater opportunity to control the ball generally and/or with spin (top or side), float, or less power (the short serve).

4. It is primarily the palm which contacts the ball. Hit the ball with a flat palm.

5. Striking the ball at its center point eliminates spin and will give the serve a knuckleball float, making it more difficult to return. Spin can be added to a serve by varying the point of contact.

Skilled servers develop a fixed rhythm to the series of actions comprising the serve (release, step, and hit). Do not discourage individual habits (e.g., giving the ball a shake, pointing the air nozzle down, and/or bouncing the ball a precise number of times) that give a player comfort in initiating the service sequence. Having a fixed or consistent serving sequence for all serves can add to the receiving team's challenge, as that team will be less able to predict the type of serve it will be facing (e.g., spinning, floating, curving, or short). This reasoning is analogous to the baseball or softball pitcher who attempts to disguise the type of pitch (e.g., fast ball, curve, knuckler, slider) to come by using the same windup each time.

Tips on Serves (Figure 2-25)

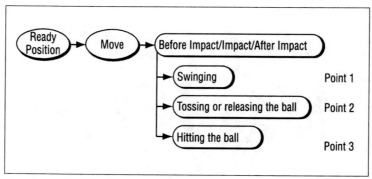

Figure 2-25. Tips on serves

Basic—Underhand Serves (Figure 2-26)

Position: The server should be facing the opponent's court.

Figure 2-26. Underhand serves (basic)

• Point 1: Swinging

As seen in Figure 2-26, the player should pull the arm in a high backward pendulum motion and then allow it to swing down and forward. Too much power causes the elbow to bend, so instruct the player to try to relax and let the arm sweep forward naturally.

• Point 2: Tossing or releasing the ball

The player should start the swing, and since there is no need to rush, take time and toss or release the ball in a relaxed, measured way.

• Point 3: Hitting the ball

In an underhand serve, contact with the ball occurs below the hips. It should be easy to visually track where the ball will be contacted, facilitating a solid hit.

Novice volleyball players most often start with the underhand serve. The ease and simplicity of the underhand technique reduces the risk of error. As an underhand serve is contacted low and with an upward and forward arm swing, there is a tendency for the serve to fly high in an arc. Although reducing service errors, underhand serves have the disadvantage of being high, slow, and easy to pass for the receiving team.

Basic—Asian Overhand Serves (Figure 2-27)

Position: The server should be perpendicular to the opponent's court, facing it side on.

Figure 2-27. Asian overhand serves (basic)

• Point 1: Swinging

The player should swing the arm from the shoulder, so that it moves as one unit (Figure 2-27). The elbow may bend slightly.

• Point 2: Tossing the ball

Tossing the ball too high will throw off timing. Players should practice their toss for consistency of height, position, timing, and coordination with the other parts of a serve. Remember that the rules of the game do not permit a second attempt to serve if the first attempt is aborted.

• Point 3: Hitting the ball

Players must keep their eyes on the ball at all times. They should set themselves up to hit the ball in the plane in front of the body. The hand can be either completely flat or lightly clenched when striking the ball for serve; the player must be careful not to overpower the hit, or the serve will fly long. Typically, players use the heel of the palm to contact the ball (Figure 2-28).

Since this serve uses mostly shoulder and hip rotation to hit the ball, even players of lesser strength can execute good serves. The player must be careful to align the body properly; it is easy to get off track when standing at an angle to the target. In addition, the player should be careful when stepping forward and swiveling the hips, as the toss may end up behind the head with the point of impact too far back. This movement could result in the ball traveling in an easily received arc or traveling in a different direction than desired.

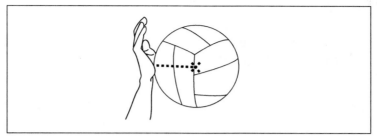
Figure 2-28. Hitting the ball with the heel of the palm

Basic—Overhand Float Serve (Figure 2-29)

Position: The server should be facing the opponent's court. Note the contrast with the Asian overhand float serve in which the non-serving side of the body faces the net.

Figure 2-29. Overhand float serve (basic)

• Point 1: Swinging

The swing for this serve is similar to the swing used in spiking. Persons with limited shoulder strength should bring their shoulder back as far as comfortably possible before hitting the ball.

• Point 2: Tossing/releasing the ball

Tossing the ball too high will throw off timing. Practicing servers should count off while drilling to learn how to transition from the toss to the impact with a constant rhythm. Another hint is to raise the tossing arm as high as possible and release the ball less than a meter aloft.

• Point 3: Hitting the ball

Practicing servers should minimize elbow bend at the moment of impact. Have players hit the ball in front of the body, generally at the highest point possible. Unlike attacks, most players hit the float serve with a locked wrist so the ball will not spin.

Because the server directly faces the opposite court, the direction of a float serve is usually stable and well controlled. This serve has less hip rotation than the Asian overhand serve, but a significant degree of upper body and shoulder strength is needed. For these reasons, volleyball players around the world with significant upper body strength frequently use the overhand float serve. Note that especially strong servers sometimes will move far back from the (end) service line so they can apply greater power and achieve more unpredictable "knuckle" or wobble in the service.

Advanced—Jump Serve (Figure 2-30)

Position: The server should face the opponent's court.

Figure 2-30. Jump serve (advanced)

• Point 1: Swinging

The jump, arm swing, wrist snap, and coordination of body actions for a jump serve closely correspond to the elements of an attack (spike).

• Point 2: Tossing

The height of the toss dictates the timing of the remaining movements of a jump serve. The toss should be to a height that feels comfortable and remains under control. Most jump servers use the same hand to toss as they use to hit the ball.

• Point 3: Hitting the ball

The player should not hit the ball down at a steep angle, as he would for an attack. Rather, the ball should be hit either parallel to the floor or slightly upward. Adjustments can be made by moving the point of impact back or forward or by reducing wrist action.

A jump serve might be considered a variation of a back row attack in which the servers set themselves behind the court end line. As with any server, the leap or takeoff to strike the serve must take place behind the end line. It is permissible for contact with the ball to occur over the court (in front of the end line) as long as the last contact with the floor occurred entirely behind the end line. Remember that the rules of the game prohibit blocking a serve. Therefore, a hard hit, spinning, or weaving serve is an offensive weapon. It is more important to pay attention to getting a solid, stable hit on the ball than to the height of the hit. To put spin on the ball, snap the wrist for a jump float, and hold the wrist steady or locked.

Ball Spin

The addition or absence of spin distinctly affects the flight of a served ball. To serve a ball without spin, the server must remember to hit it dead on at the center point. Striking the ball even a little off center will add spin. Spiked or served balls will tend to curve in the direction of the spin; greater spin increases the tendency of the ball to curve. Conversely, balls hit without spin become extremely susceptible to fluctuations in air currents and movement brought about by drag on minute imperfections in the shape of every ball. Serves without spin can behave unpredictably (the knuckle ball effect), making them more difficult to receive.

Serves with spin move in a predetermined direction due to what is called the Magnus effect. If a passer can determine the direction the ball is spinning, she can predict the way it will move. A server or spiker can easily add spin to a ball by moving the hitting hand off the ball's center point, turning the wrist in the direction of the desired spin, and adding force (Figure 2-31).

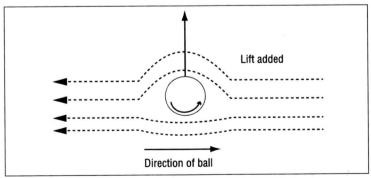

Figure 2-31. Effects of spin on the serve

Practice Drills

Basic—Chant Serve (Figure 2-32)

When serving, the player should always try to hit the ball with the same rhythm, so that the height of the toss and the speed of the service movements will be consistent. Have the player practice counting off when serving, with one for when starting to move, two for the toss, and three for the moment of contact with the ball.

Figure 2-32. Chant serve (basic)

Basic—Bounce Serve (Figure 2-33)

Have a partner loop the ball over the server from behind. The server should practice hitting serves as the ball rebounds from the floor. Adjust the height and speed of the looping throws so the ball will bounce to the level of a toss.

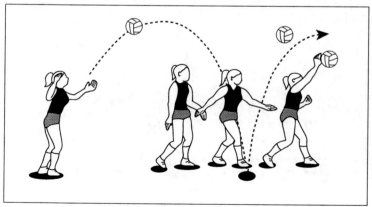

Figure 2-33. Bounce serve (basic)

Basic—Colored Ball Serve

To see and understand spin on a ball, have the players practice serving with a multi-colored ball. The server should watch the ball to observe the spin of different types of serves based on power applied, location of contact with the ball, wrist snap, and other variables. In this way, players will discover which serves they are able to make most effectively and consistently. Tachikara, Mikasa, Molten, Spalding, and other prominent volleyball manufacturers offer colored balls that would be perfect for this purpose.

The Block

Blocks are the first line of defense against an opposing team on the attack. Mastering the elements of blocking—including the correct position to jump, arm extension, and timing—leads to a more offensive defense. Limiting an opponent's attack through an effective or well-placed block makes it easier for backcourt diggers to position themselves for an accurate pass. Blocking too often is an undervalued skill. At the same time, blocking is a difficult skill, as it takes place immediately next to the net. Touching the net during the play of the ball results in a fault (and a point for the opposing team).

Fundamentals of Blocking

The following numbers correspond to the numbers in Figure 2-34:

1. When the opponents have the ball, front row players should be ready to block with knees bent and arms extended up in front of their head, with the fingers open, in the shape of the ball.

Figure 2-34. Fundamentals of blocking

2. After determining from where on the net the attack will come, step out with the foot that leads in (closest to) that direction and move to the optimal blocking position (a whole separate science determined by the number of blockers, design of the defense, and other variables). Depending on the set, some lateral moves are short, and a single side step is sufficient; other moves are longer and require practice in smooth and quick lateral movement.
3. Plant both feet after the lateral move, bend the knees, watch the set and the attacker's approach, and, with practiced timing, jump.
4. Extend hands and arms up and forward as if skimming them along the net.
5. As a blocker clears the net, she should tense hands, elbows, chin, and stomach, and thrust the shoulders upward. This technique has the effect of "piking" or extending the hands and arms (if the player is physically gifted with a good jump) over the net.

Players should land with an awareness of where the ball was hit or blocked, and be prepared to block again immediately (if the first ball was successfully blocked) or to assist with the defense, set, or spike.

Tips on Blocking (Figure 2-35)

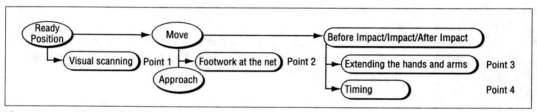

Figure 2-35. Tips on blocking

• Point 1: Visual scanning

Keeping the attacker within the field of vision, a blocker's eyes should scan and focus in this order: ball, setter, ball, attacker. A focus limited to the ball ignores an attacker's angle of approach—a critical variable when deciding where to block. The blocker should keep the field of vision wide, and he should practice keeping the ball in the field of vision while looking at the attacker, and the attacker in the field of vision while looking at the ball.

• Point 2: Footwork at the net (Figure 2-36)

Blockers should lead (move first) with the foot that is closest to the direction of the intended block (i.e., step out with the right foot when moving to the right and with the left foot when moving left). This (most efficient) technique accelerates movement to the location of an intended block. To the extent reasonably possible, blockers should try to move with their knees slightly bent in a loaded position and their arms raised.

Figure 2-36. Footwork at the net

• Point 3: Extending the hands and arms

When jumping, blockers should extend their hands and arms up along the net and forward. Once the arms have cleared the net, they should further reduce the attacker's space to adjust a hit by bending the hands forward at the wrist with fingers splayed (spread as wide as possible). When the attacker hits the ball, blockers should not wave their arms (Figure 2-37). Rather, blockers should hold their arms up close against their heads, using the chest, shoulder, and arm muscles to stiffen or strengthen the block (Figure 2-38). As blockers play more experienced opponents, they will encounter hitters who try to wipe the ball off the block (hit the ball sideways off the blocker's hands and out-of-bounds). Correspondingly, more experienced outside blockers learn to turn the hand nearest the sideline slightly in to defeat any wipe attempt and increase the probability of blocking the ball into the opponent's court.

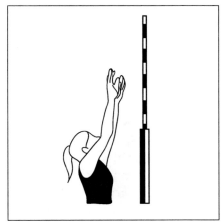 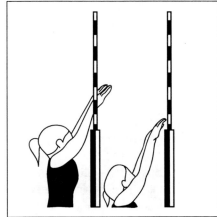

Figure 2-37. Incorrect arm placement   Figure 2-38. Correct arm placement

- Point 4: Timing

To block an attacker receiving a quick or low set, the blocker should jump at about the same time as the attacker. To block an attacker receiving a higher set, the blocker should jump slightly after the attacker. To block a backcourt attack, the blocker should jump after the attacker contacts the ball.

Practice Drills

Basic—Jumping Form

- Jump in place, straight up, practicing proper form (for hands, arms, shoulders, etc.).
- Practice moving a step to either side and jumping with proper blocking form.
- Practice moving a distance of three meters and jumping with proper form.

Basic—Timing and Footwork (Figure 2-39)

Have a partner toss a ball over the net from the opposite court setter position (middle front), and have the player jump to block it.

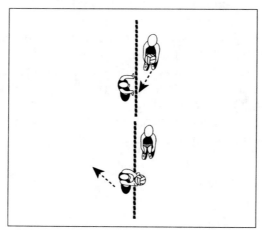

Figure 2-39. Timing and footwork (basic)

Basic—Visual Scanning

Have the blocker stand opposite the net from a partner. Starting at the same position as the setter, the blocker should practice blocking attacks that the partner hits from two-meter high tosses. The attacker should hit in the direction the blocker is moving. In this way, the blocker must concentrate on blocking into (turning the hands down and toward the middle of) the court, as the hit ball otherwise will carom off a flat block and out-of-bounds.

3

Building the Game

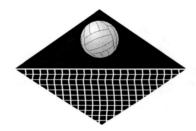

This chapter explains the basics of developing the individual skills that bring a game to life, including a variety of attacks.

Understanding How Plays Unfold
(Technical Framework)

A volleyball can be played (touched) three times when it crosses into a team's side of the court. The first play is the reception (receiving a serve or spike), the second is the set and the third is the attack. These actions constitute the basic plays of volleyball and offensive strategy involves the knowledge and application of their variations. Under six-player rules, a block is not considered one of the three permitted contacts by a team before the ball must be returned to the opponent's court. In other words, a team may play or touch the ball three times after contacting it for a block. Note that a team need not touch or contact the ball three times before returning it to the opposing court. A receiving player sometimes will immediately return a ball to an open area of an opponent's court on the first ball (direct attack) or a player will attack with a second contact (second touch attack).

To complete these plays requires proper technical skills. These fundamental skills are: serving, overhand passing, underhand passing, attacking, and blocking.

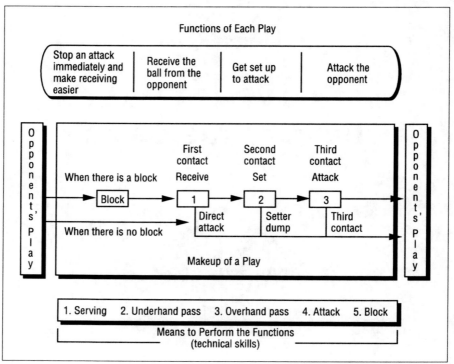

Figure 3-1. Framework of volleyball skills

Receiving (First Contact)

The first handling of a serve or attack from an opponent involves the action or skills of reception, passing, or digging. An opponent's serve or attack may come in an infinite variety of forms: fast, hard, spinning, floating/knuckling, deep, short, soft, high, or in a combination of such characteristics. The receiving team strives to prevent the ball from touching the court surface to avoid a point for the opponent. Players making first contact with the ball endeavor to direct the ball in a manner that makes it easy for the setter to handle the ball on the second contact and gives the setter the most options for delivering or setting the ball to an attacker. A poor pass often reduces the quality of a set, which follows or forces the setter to set in only one (predictable to the defense) direction. To become proficient in receiving, practice the appropriate ready positions and learn to shift as necessary from those positions for the serve receive or the attack receive.

BEING READY AND MOVING

To receive well, players must be prepared to react quickly to the many varieties of serves and attacks. As movement to the ball is a common player deficiency, remind players of the obvious: the goal of the offense is to "hit 'em where they ain't!" Such preparation necessitates paying attention to proper arm position, line of sight, and the angle of the knees. The next step is moving quickly to where the ball will come down. Many patterns or methods may be employed for moving; practice all of them to develop the ability to use the most appropriate technique for a given situation. Finally, a player must be able to determine quickly which platform (overhand or underhand) will legally direct (without lifting or throwing) the ball to its target accurately.

Ready Position

In Figure 3-2, the player's heels are flat on the floor. Even though this is a stable and comfortable position, it is not appropriate for moving quickly to receive the ball. Shifting from a stable or flat-footed position to movement requires a shift in posture *before* the movement which, therefore, delays the response time. In other words, being prepared to respond rapidly requires being in an unstable stance, rather than a stable one. Becoming accustomed to the "ready" stance for receiving serves or spikes requires practice as the position is difficult to maintain for any length of time without repetition.

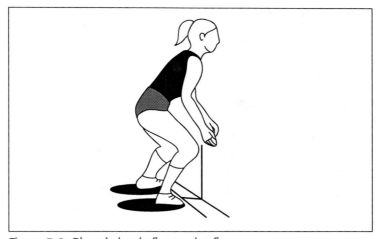

Figure 3-2. Player's heels flat on the floor

Figure 3-3 depicts the normal reception stance. In that stance, a player should maintain a low line of vision, bent knees, and low center of gravity to facilitate quick response to a spike or serve. The feet should be slightly more than shoulder-width apart but not too far apart. As mentioned above, a receiver's heels should be off the floor. In the "ready" stance, the knees should be in front of the toes, which position automatically pulls the heels off the floor. Receiver response to a high ball will be too slow if the hands are too low, so they should be kept at chest level. In practice, have someone check to ensure a player's stance matches the position depicted in Figure 3-3.

Figure 3-3. Reception stance

Moving on the Court

Servers and spikers rarely (and only accidentally) hit a ball directly to a receiver/passer. Consequently, passers most often will have to move to receive the ball. A player must be able to shift rapidly and precisely to move under the ball to maximize the probability of an accurate and legal pass. Generally, the two different ways to shift are side-shuffle stepping and turn-and-run. Players should learn both methods of moving to a ball.

Figure 3-4 shows the side-shuffle step. This quick, lateral movement is used when the ball is coming to a point fairly close to the passer. The crossover or turn-and-run step in Figure 3-5 is for balls that are farther away. Absent a high, looping free ball, players should always use the side-shuffle step to begin moving toward an incoming ball. The side-shuffle step moves a passer to the ball, maintaining most elements of the proper receiving stance, while the crossover step requires temporary abandonment

Figure 3-4. Side-shuffle step

of the stance. The shuffle step tends to inhibit a player's center of gravity from shifting up or down too much while moving. If the ball comes to a player's right, he should first step with the right foot; if it comes to the left, the first step is with the left foot. If the ball is heading toward the back part of the court, a passer should move backward first with a backpedal or drop step.

Figure 3-5. Crossover (turn-and-run) step

The crossover step is used to move backward on a diagonal, as shown in Figure 3-6. A player should practice maintaining a frontal view of the net during this angled movement to the ball.

Figure 3-6. Crossover step backward on a diagonal

Practice Points and Drills

Practice Points:

- Remain in a relaxed, ready position from which to respond rapidly.
- Shift in a manner that maintains an uninterrupted view of the ball.

Basic—Movement Practice Using the Net

Players usually need to practice both of the explained movements and maintaining line of sight. As shown in Figure 3-7, players should line up their eyes with the lower part of the net and practice moving with the side-shuffle step or the crossover step, without changing their line of sight.

Figure 3-7. The line of sight should line up with the bottom of the net.

Advanced—Rebound Receive (Figure 3-8)

The player should stand, facing the wall, and prepare to receive. Another person should throw the ball over the passer's shoulder from behind. The passer should either catch or receive the ball as it rebounds. As the passer improves, he should focus exclusively on moving to the ball and passing it with proper form and direction. Adjust the passer's position relative to the wall and the speed of the thrown ball to match their skill level.

Figure 3-8. Rebound receive (advanced)

RECEIVING A SERVE

On every rally, the first play for the team not serving is serve receive. Serve receive and, indeed, receiving/passing generally is considered the most important skill in the game, as that skill impacts the quality of the set and spike that ideally follow. If a team fails to receive the serve properly, the serving team immediately receives a point. Receiving a serve uses the same basic technique as an underhand pass. The primary difference between the skills lies in the amount of time and distance covered by the served or spiked ball. A passer has more time to adjust or react to a served ball than to a spiked ball. Conversely, a served ball has more time to flutter, spin, curve, and otherwise make it difficult for a receiving player to pass well.

Skills Employed in Serve Receive

During the process of receiving a serve, a player must first estimate where the served ball will fall (in or out, high or low, where on the court). A passer then must determine who is responsible for covering the area of the court where the ball is falling and whether that player is aware and prepared to pass. A player should never assume another player is prepared to pass and always be prepared to assist or even take the pass. Assuming a passer has responsibility for an incoming serve, he must move quickly to the area of the incoming ball, get into a receiving stance, make contact with the ball, and follow through. The process of passing can be divided into three steps, as shown in Figure 3-9. All three steps must be executed smoothly. Step 2 requires more practice than the other steps. Good position and stance to play the ball lead toward more and consistent precision when contacting the ball in the third stage. Passing is a rhythmic process, and the best rhythm emphasizes the second step.

Figure 3-9. Three-step passing process

Step 1: Once the ball is served, judge the angle and speed. Predict where it will fall and as soon as possible, take the first step. Then, move with knees slightly bent and avoiding any up-down head movements.

Step 2: Once in position where the ball will fall, clasp the hands together and prepare for contact. Draw in the chin, and glance upward to see the bottom of the ball. Place either foot forward, and turn the toes of the forward foot, the midline of the body, and the forearms to face the setter.

Step 3: While straightening the elbows, contact the ball on the forearm within two inches of the wrist. Bend the knee of the front leg forward, and push forward with the entire body as though lifting the ball. Do not swing the arms, as all but the softest serves have sufficient energy to rebound from the passer's arms to the setter. Adding force with an arm swing too often results in an overpass to the delight of the opposing front row.

Points to Check in Receiving Serves

- Be ready in a relaxed position, but stay prepared.
- Move swiftly without moving the head too much.
- Angle arms toward the setter (this point is very important).
- Ideally, meet the ball in about the middle part of the body.
- Shift body weight onto the front foot.

Practice Points and Drills

Practice Points:

- Be sure to have the entire platform facing the setter.
- Look at the underside of the ball without moving the head too much.
- As much as possible, use the lower body (especially the knees) to propel the ball into the air.

Basic—Two Players, No Net (Figure 3-10)

Standing five to six meters apart, one player should serve underhand to the other player. The second player should catch the ball and immediately serve it again. The player should try to receive the ball as close to his midline as possible, and should receive the ball with enough strength (from the compressed energy of the bent knees and ankles and the slight forward motion of the body) to return the ball to the first player in one touch. This repetitive drill develops passing rhythm.

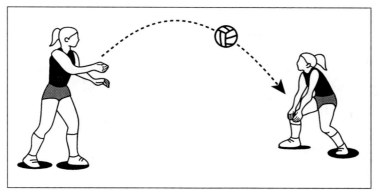

Figure 3-10. Two players, no net (basic)

Advanced—Two Players, No Net (Figure 3-11)

The player should move backward down the court while receiving the serve. The two players should increase the distance between them and move a few steps back after passing the ball. In this drill, the server delivers a ball slightly deeper than the position of the passer. The passer should focus on learning to move backward (through drop steps) while maintaining concentration on the airborne ball and on shifting his entire body forward when contacting the ball. Players should begin the backward movement with the foot that was farther back when positioned to receive the serve.

Figure 3-11. Two players, no net (advanced)

Basic—Two Players With Net (Figure 3-12)

Two players stand on the same side of the net in staggered forward/back position, ready to receive the serve. A third player or coach serves over the net. The passers should take turns passing in the front or back position so both gain experience passing short and deeper serves. In addition, passers in this drill should work on communicating

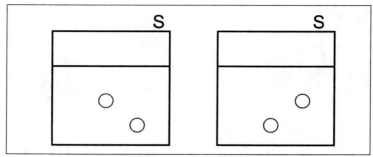

Figure 3-12. Two players with net (basic)

with each other and opening up (non-passer turning toward the other player) to support or assist the passer.

This drill strives to make players decide whether to receive the serve or let someone else receive it as players are moving into receiving position. If a player tries to decide before moving, his response will be too slow, and the player generally will not be in position to receive the serve. Players should determine who will (or should) receive the serve while starting to move. Players should develop the habit of communicating whether they will receive the serve or let the adjacent player take it. Once a ball is served, *all* players should move to pass, to assist the player determined to be the optimum passer for the situation, to set, and/or to spike a set.

RECEIVING AN ATTACK OR DIGGING

A team that cannot receive an opponent's attack (consistently passing the ball with reasonable control and direction so the setter has a chance to place the ball where an attacker can spike it) will not be able to mount a successful attack. Accordingly, receiving or digging an attack is fully as important as receiving a serve. In contrast with a serve initiated behind the end line and which must travel generally two-thirds to four-fifths the length of the court, an attack (spike) generally is made at, and above the height of, the net. Consequently, attacked balls travel much faster than serves and with significantly greater downward trajectory. Passers, therefore, have little time to prepare for an attack, but, rather, must react and make split-second decisions how to move. An art or skill is developed through experience of reading the opposing setter and/or hitters to determine where the set likely will be delivered and from where the attack will come. Successful anticipation slightly increases the time the passer has to react to an attack, as the passer will have moved closer to where the spike likely will originate and land. Experienced passers also incorporate the additional factor of adjusting to their team's block (i.e., assuming with cautious trust the block will take away a spiker's ability to hit into the court behind the block, thereby freeing the receiver to cover more of the open court). To dig an attack, players must practice and master the skills of creating an effective platform with their arms, understanding how to control the ball's momentum, and the emergency reaction techniques of diving and rolling.

Skills Employed in Receiving Attacks

Overhand Style

When receiving an attack, players must deal with extremely fast balls, so it is most common to use an underhand receive. Until relatively recent changes in the rules of the game, players most often used the grip illustrated in Figure 3-13 to receive balls above the shoulder. Because the rules now allow multiple contacts using finger action in a single attempt to play the ball, receives or dig/pass attempts of hard-driven attacks that cause the ball to bounce between fingers or hands are no longer deemed illegal double contacts. As a result, it is now possible to use an overhand pass technique to receive an attack or serve. Note that a first-ball lift or carry remains illegal; the rule change permitting multiple-contact first balls has created some referee leniency here, too.

Figure 3-13. Hand clasp once used to receive balls above the shoulder

Underhand Style

Even with good ready position and rapid response, if a player cannot make a proper platform with his arms, that player will not be able to dig well. Players can use the grip (hand clasp for establishing a platform) for serve receive underhand passes as a reference, but should learn and practice a grip they can make quickly. An effective platform includes lining up the arms with the incoming ball and mentally calculating incoming and rebound angles to create an accurate pass to the setter. Players develop the ability to judge angle, speed, and alignment only through many repetitions in practice.

Figure 3-14 illustrates the principle of aligning the platform. As shown in the bottom image of the figure, the momentum of the ball cannot be stopped if the arms are closed, in which case the ball will usually shoot off at an angle at high speed (a "shanked" pass). Players who get under the ball can volley it straight up, as shown at the top of the figure.

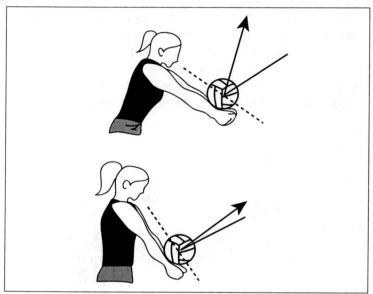

Figure 3-14. Correct (top) and incorrect (bottom) platform alignment for getting under the ball

To dig an attack successfully, a player must make the correct platform in a split second and then face the platform toward the target (usually the setter). If a player uses the same ready position for balls coming on the left or right, his stance will resemble the one pictured in the bottom image of Figure 3-15. This form creates an upward angled or flat platform, which will cause the ball to shoot to the side or backward. To avoid shanking the ball, the outer or upper arm should slightly overlap higher than the inner or lower one, and the platform should be fine tuned to match the one pictured at the top of Figure 3-15. Such adjustments must be made instantly, which is one of the reasons digging is such a difficult skill to master and maintain.

Ball Control for Hard Driven Spikes

Two methods for stopping the momentum of a ball are outlined in Figure 3-16. The first is to create a cushion with the compressed "spring" of the arms. The second is bending the knees when digging. These methods create a cushion that absorbs some of the energy of a hard-driven ball. Both methods can be used together for really hard-

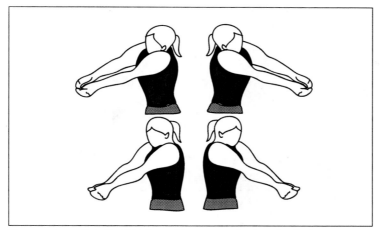

Figure 3-15. Correct (top) and incorrect (bottom) platform alignment for lining up the arms with the incoming ball

driven balls. Through repetitions in practice, passers' bodies learn to conform naturally to the momentum of the ball. When able to dig in a relaxed state, receivers can pass balls hit forcefully or softly.

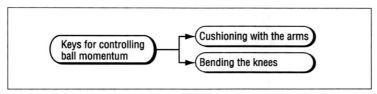

Figure 3-16. Stopping ball momentum

Dives and Extension Roll Receives

Players dive or roll to receive or simply (desperately) contact balls dropping far from their ready position, and often coming down so quickly that they do not have time to move to get under the ball with a proper platform. Although dives and rolls can be breathtaking athletic plays, it always is preferable to move to an incoming ball and create a proper platform. Too frequently, a dive or roll becomes necessary because a player begins moving toward a driven ball too late or too slowly. In the past, men usually used dives (Figure 3-17) and women usually used extension rolls (Figure 3-18). Now, athletes of both genders utilize the techniques equally. Diving and rolling are physically dynamic skills that can cause injury if not practiced and perfected. It is natural for a player to feel some fear or intimidation when first learning the skills. In such situations, it can relieve or reduce such hesitation by having a player start to learn from a kneeling position.

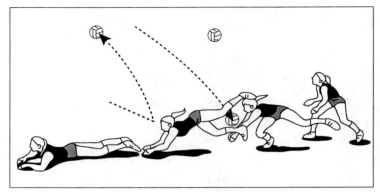

Figure 3-17. Dive

Figure 3-18. Extension roll

Practice Points and Drills

Practice Points:

- Become able to make the proper platform in a split second.
- Become able to absorb or greatly reduce the momentum of the ball.
- Become able to pass the ball in a controlled manner to the setter or another target on the court.

Basic—Kneeling Receive (Figure 3-19)

The passer should prepare to dig in the kneeling position. Have someone hit the ball from four or five meters away (or have them throw the ball), and practice bumping the ball straight up in the air. Start by having the hitter/tosser hit directly to the kneeling passer. As the passer develops skill and confidence, have the second player hit the ball an increasing distance from the (still kneeling) passer. The increasing distance will teach the passer to dive or roll without fear, eventually enabling the passer to practice from a (standing) ready position.

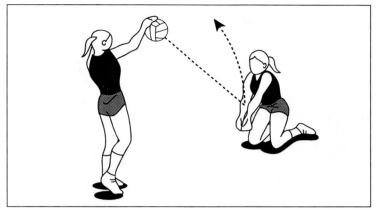

Figure 3-19. Kneeling receive (basic)

Advanced—Receiving a Spike (Figure 3-20)

Have the passer assume the ready position with his entire body relaxed. The passer should practice digging (reacting to) a ball a partner or coach spikes straight at the passer as hard as possible from two or three meters away. At first, the passer should only concentrate on body and platform so the ball strikes his forearms. If a passer is tense, the ball will rebound too hard. This drill should help the passer learn to absorb some of the power from a hard-drive ball and develop quicker reaction time to increase the accuracy and control of the pass.

Figure 3-20. Receiving a spike (advanced)

Setting (Second Contact)

A good set gives the attackers a ball that is easy to attack, maximizes the options available to the attacker (where on the court the attacker can direct the ball), and/ or sets up an attack for which the defense is less prepared (or unprepared). A set is generally the second of only three allowable contacts by a team before which the ball must be directed across the net to the opposing court. Beginning or lesser skilled teams often have difficulty passing accurately or setting well, rendering a three-touch attack difficult or ineffective. Even if only one player on the team can set well, the whole team can be galvanized, and volleyball will become fun. A skilled setter often can translate a poor or mediocre pass into a reasonable or even well placed set, giving a hitter a realistic opportunity to score.

Most sets utilize the skill of overhand passing. Unusually low or shanked passes sometimes necessitate underhand or forearm sets (bump sets). As with passing, overhand sets are preferred because of the greater ball control.

As the term denotes, setters deliver most of a team's sets during a game (confusingly, games are also known as sets). The setter usually receives and sets the ball near the net, about one-third to halfway down the net from the right side. This positioning near the net requires setters to master a different set of skills than the players defending an open court or hitting a strategically placed set.

Proper Setting Movement (Stance)

Setters (or, indeed, anyone setting the ball for a hitter) should get into the proper position before setting a ball. Proper position involves quickly moving beneath the incoming ball, endeavoring to receive the ball within an imaginary funnel, the bottom of which would point at the setter's upper-middle forehead. The funnel, in turn, is the same area through which the setter propels or directs the outgoing set in front, behind, or even to the side. The second and third positions in Figure 3-21 show the proper setting position. This position must be visible to passers so they have a target and to attackers so they know to anticipate a possible set. To achieve this, as mentioned before, setters must move under the ball/pass as quickly as possible, so they have some leeway for adjustments. Quick positioning under the pass facilitates a setter being able to raise his arms before the ball descends too low.

Get the arms and elbows up as early as possible. Elbows should be higher than the shoulders.

Ensure enough leeway.

Body weight should be on the balls of the feet.

Point the toes at the target of the set.

Place one foot ahead of the other.

Figure 3-21. Proper setting position

Setting Techniques

Setting techniques vary. However, they all tend to share the qualities of keeping the elbows and knees bent, catching the ball at the lowest point of a squat, and straightening the arms and knees to set the ball. Technique differences relate to the tempo of stretching up from the squat, set stance, and ball direction.

Tempo

- Basic—Slow tempo sets usually require slow straightening of elbows and knees (Figure 3-22).

Figure 3-22. Slow tempo set (basic)

- Advanced—Fast tempo sets usually require quick straightening of elbows and knees (Figure 3-23).

Figure 3-23. Fast tempo set (advanced)

Stance

Basic—Back set (Figure 3-24)

Basic—Jump set (Figure 3-25)

Advanced—Roll set (Figure 3-26)

Advanced—Side set (Figures 3-27 and 3-28)

The entire body leans backward.
Catch the ball directly above the head.

Passing forward from this position is also permitted.

Figure 3-24. Back set (basic)

Figure 3-25. Jump set (basic)

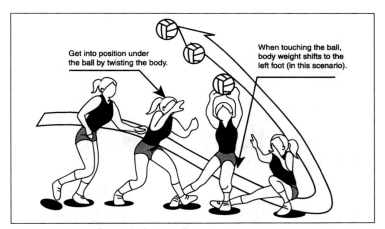

Figure 3-26. Roll set (advanced)

Figure 3-27. Side set—back to the net (advanced)

Figure 3-28. Side set—facing the net (advanced)

Practice Points and Drills

Practice Points:

- Get into position under the ball as quickly as possible, facing the target.
- Master the methods of catching, releasing, and accurately directing the ball so attackers can easily hit the set.

Basic—Bounce set

The setter should practice getting under the ball, no matter what kind of ball it is, and allow for some leeway before the ball falls. The setter can start by practicing setting using his head (Figure 3-29), then move on to regular sets from this same position (Figure 3-30).

Figure 3-29. Bounce set (basic) using the head

Figure 3-30. Bounce set (basic) using the hands

Basic—Digging and Setting

The coach or attacker spikes the ball over the net to a player (receiver) who digs (passes) the ball up to another player (setter) who sets (overhand pass) toward the left front for an attack (Figure 3-31).

This drill may be varied by changing the following elements:
- Coach's position or receiver's position (the source of the ball to be received)
- Height of the dug ball
- Starting position of the setter
- Type of set (first tempo, second tempo, third tempo)
- Set techniques (back set, jump set, etc.)

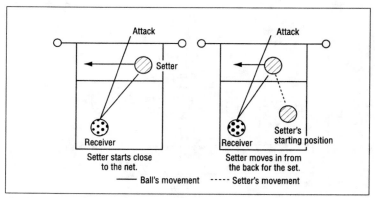

Figure 3-31. Digging and setting (basic)

Basic—Silent Pass

A coach tosses the ball to the setter without saying anything to the attackers. This drill compels the setter to choose the attacker and helps the attackers learn where (and how) a setter will or can deliver the ball when it is passed in certain ways (high, low, fast) and/or to certain areas of the front row.

Advanced—Willow Pass (Figure 3-32)

The willow pass is so-called because the wrists droop like a willow tree. To increase setter flexibility, have him assume the ready position with wrists bent (relaxed completely). This drill forces the setter to move his wrists from completely relaxed and drooping to the proper basket position under the incoming (tossed) ball.

Figure 3-32. Willow pass (advanced)

Basic—Parallel Pass

A set ball delivered to the middle of an attacker's approach is the attacker's worst nightmare as it abbreviates the approach, reduces or eliminates the jump, could cause the hitter to hit from under (rather than behind) the ball, and limits hitting options. The optimal delivery point is the end of an attacker's approach, such as in front of, and above, where the attacker will be after maximizing speed and jumping force at the conclusion of a full approach and in a location where the attacker will not be trapped against the opposing team's block (Figure 3-33). Therefore, setters should pay attention to the following:

- Make sure palms are properly facing the target.
- Make sure to balance (equalize) the amount of force used to set the ball between both arms.
- Set with one foot behind the body for greater balance and thrust (in Figure 3-33, it is the left foot).
- After setting the ball, move to cover the spiker in case the hit is blocked.

In Figure 3-34, a set is shown from above. Note the sequence between waiting to receive the pass and release or delivery of the ball.

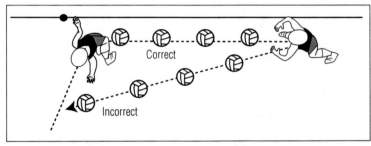

Figure 3-33. Set with one foot behind the body

Figure 3-34. Set (shown from above)

Advanced—Backspin Set

The purpose of this backspin drill is to practice giving the attacker an easy-to-hit ball. If the set has topspin, the highest point of the ball's trajectory will tend to fall short of the attacker, as illustrated in Figure 3-35. This ball will be difficult for an attacker to hit. However, if the ball is given a backspin, the highest point will be closer to the attacker's position, and it will descend (desirably) in front of the attacker. This kind of ball is easy to hit. The easiest ball to hit is actually one with no spin. By practicing how to set with a backspin, setters learn greater overall ball control and better master the techniques of effective setting.

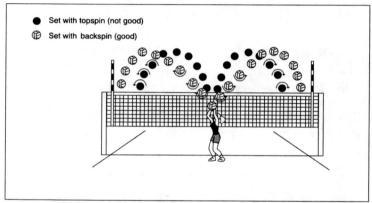

Figure 3-35. Comparison of sets with topspin (not good) and backspin (good)

Attack (Third Contact)

The attack (spike) requires the most aggressive elements of all volleyball skills. Attacks vary greatly by approach, takeoff, impact force, and midair movements or adjustments. By learning to vary these aspects of an attack, hitters become less predictable, less defensible, and, therefore, more successful. Moreover, by matching the height, length, and speed of the set, hitters increase the effectiveness of their attacks. Experienced hitters learn to coordinate with the setter and other attackers to create combination attacks (two or more hitters leaping together or consecutively in the same play), making it difficult for blockers to determine whom they should block and for defenders to decide where to cover.

Attacking Techniques

Hits

The types of hits can be classified into the categories presented in Figure 3-36. Types of placement (i.e., where to target a hit) are shown in Figure 3-37. The tendency is to think only about attacking on the horizontal axis, such as the common crosscourt, straight (down the line), or cutback shots. Many other variations using vertical placements can be used to achieve the number-one goal in attacking: hitting a ball the opponent cannot receive (or, at least, cannot pass easily). The 12-meter mark in Figure 3-38 represents the target of the attack; in this attack, the hitter aims the spike high so it flies off the top of the blocker's hands and lands "out" beyond the end line. This hit is known as a (deep) wipe-off. Aiming for the nine-meter mark would be hitting balls deep on the court, six meters would be hitting mid-court, and three meters would be sharp attacks near the net.

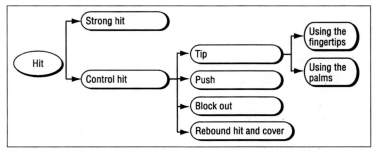

Figure 3-36. Types of hits

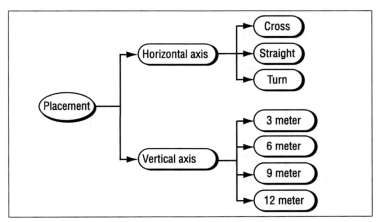

Figure 3-37. Types of placement

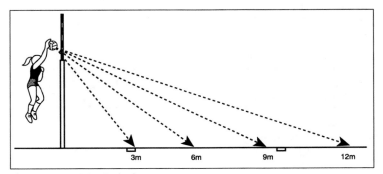

Figure 3-38. Vertical placements

A variation of the wipe attack has the hitter aim for the outside edge of a blocker's hands so the touched ball lands out-of-bounds. An advanced technique of wipe attack is sometimes applied by experienced hitters when the set is tight (close to the plane of the net), and the hitter knows he might be trapped in a stuff block. Anticipating that the blocker(s) will be all over the ball so close to (or in) the plane of the net, the hitter will take a normal approach and then shift the hitting hand to strike the ball from the side, attempting to hit the ball almost parallel to the net off the blocker's hands and out-of-bounds. The wipe attack is one of the reasons coaches remind and drill the outside blocker (closest to the sideline) to turn the outside hand in and down toward the court to ensure any blocked balls land in.

Approaches

The movement or transition from the starting position to hit the ball where the set will come down is called the "approach." Typical approaches are summarized in Figure 3-39 and illustrated in Figure 3-40. The numbers in the following list correspond to the numbers in Figure 3-40. Novice to intermediate hitters should master approaches 1, 2, and 3. Ambitious and experienced players should challenge themselves and learn approaches 4 and 5.

1. Straight: This most basic approach comes straight at the net parallel to the sideline.
2. Angle: This approach comes at the net in a straight diagonal. This approach is used for the (most common) crosscourt outside attack.
3. Loop or Swing: The path of this approach looks like an arc. It is used when making an open attack from either the left or the right side. Left- or right-side hitters use this approach to maintain greater flexibility to hit down the line or crosscourt.
4. Slide (Figure 3-41): This approach starts off by running either left or right parallel to the net, then turning and approaching the net from an angle. It concludes with a quick attack, using a one-legged takeoff. This approach is very similar to a lay-up in basketball. Very often, the hitter involved in a slide play starts on one side of the setter, transitions along the net (behind the setter at the net) to the other side of the setter, and then turns to hit a lateral set a yard or two away from the setter.

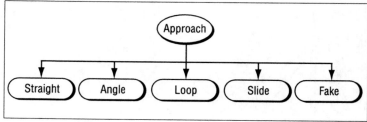

Figure 3-39. Types of approach patterns

5. Fake: This approach starts off the same as a loop. During the approach, the athlete quickly changes direction. This approach is especially good for a stack attack (moving directly behind another hitter and jumping fractionally after the other/front hitter so the setter has the option of a short, quick one-foot-above-the-net set to the first hitter, who might draw the block, or a slower, two- or three-foot-high set slightly off the net for the second hitter, who might have no block), or when pretending to hit a front one (again, a quick low set in front of the setter) but actually hitting a back two (akin to a slide).

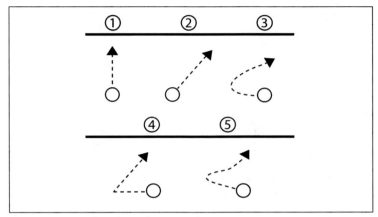

Figure 3-40. Examples of approach patterns

Figure 3-41. Slide approach

Takeoffs

Many methods can be used for taking off or leaping to spike a set (Figure 3-42), including:

- Slide (Figure 3-43): Players hitting a slide attack take off on one foot as the horizontal slide approach concludes with a sharp turn toward the net to hit a low set.
- Single pump attacks: There are two different types of single pump attacks. In the first type, hitters approach the A quick attack position, fake a jump by straightening out the arms (down and slightly behind, as though prepared to throw them into the air for maximum lift), and slightly straightening the legs, then bending them and jumping again from the same place. The other method of pump attack is to fake a jump, quickly change places (by slide, turn of the body, or otherwise), and then hit the ball.

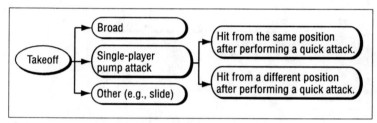

Figure 3-42. Types of takeoffs

Figure 3-43. Slide attack

Types of Sets

Open Set (Second-Stage Set)

The open set (high and usually outside) is used when the first contact does not pass the ball to a position where the setter feels able to try a quick, back, or complicated play set (i.e., where the setter must employ the least complicated, safest set to avoid mishandling the poor pass). Additionally, when a team lacks the skill or experience to use quick attacks, second tempo, time-differential attacks, or pump attacks, most all attacks are some form of an open set. There are usually three positions for open sets: left, center, and right. Second-stage sets are not limited to the front line. On occasion, the easiest available set (outlet or safety set) is to a back row player. For example, when the first contact flies outside the right sideline and the setter is in the right front, rather than sending the left front a long open set, the more appropriate tactic might be an accurate open set to the right back.

Combination Attack

The following three dimensions, all of which are dependent on the setter, define combination attacks:

- Vertical (length) or distance from the net (back line attacks, etc.)
- Horizontal (width) or position along the net
- Altitude or height above the top of the net

Figure 3-44 summarizes typical attacks used for various attack tempos, which are determined by the set height and speed. Figure 3-45a illustrates all three dimensions of combination attacks. Figures 3-45b through 3-45d show other examples of offensive systems that can be created to identify and define the height, distance, and depth of sets used in an offensive system.

Tempo	Set Height	Typical Attacks
First tempo	0 to 2 meters	A, B, C, or D quick attack
Second tempo	2 to 4 meters	Pump attack, left front shoot or go, back shoot or go, time-differential attacks
Third tempo	4 to 6 meters	Open set

Figure 3-44. Attack tempos

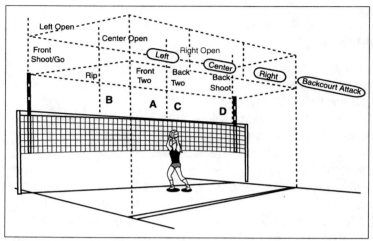

Figure 3-45a. Attacking system (similar to USA 2004 system)

3rd tempo 80cm = 33 inch	53	43	33	23	13	03	a3	b3	c3
2nd tempo 80cm = 33 inch	52	42	32	22	12	02	a2	b2	c2
1st tempo 80cm = 33 inch	5	4	3	2	1	0 Setter	a	b	c

Figure 3-45b. Front row attack number/letter system

high								high
Neptune	Jupiter	Mars	Moon			Venus	Mercury	
			wide	tight	Earth Setter	back tight	back wide	

Figure 3-45c. Front row attack nicknames

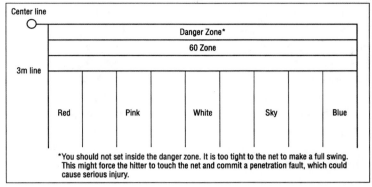

Figure 3-45d. Back row attack nicknames

Practice Drills

Basic—Straight-Up Set Attack

Have the hitters practice shot placement from straight-up sets. Identify a target (such as a position number on the court), and have the players try to hit it. An interesting variation is to place a moderately heavy target that will roll (such as a medicine ball), and then have the hitters attempt to roll it off the court by hitting it. A further variation would be to divide the team into two equally skilled hitting lines with one line on each side of the net and a medicine ball placed in the same position on each court; have the two teams compete to see who can hit/move the ball off the court first.

Advanced—Hit Two Balls in Succession

Have a hitter attack from the serve receive position (back row attack) and then hit a high ball at the net. The setter should signal (alert) the spiker before setting for the back row. Similarly, the spiker should give the setter an audible signal (call for the ball) prior to receiving the free ball. The purposes of this drill are to develop in hitters the ability to transition quickly from one play to an attack and to improve and increase communication between teammates.

Playing a Game—Basics of Setting Up Attacks

Before playing a real game with all rules enforced, it is imperative for teams to practice mock games and diverse game situations so players become familiar with teammate movements and reactions to various situations. Rather than enforcing the rules of the game strictly, it is advisable to practice games or game situations that match the players' technical level.

Volleyball is the ultimate team game. Outside the rare service ace or single stuff block, it is impossible for one player to score without teammate assistance. As in any sport, volleyball has its stars and players who possess greater skills than others. In nearly every rally, however, teammates must take their turns serving, passing the ball, setting the ball, participating in a block, faking or taking a hit, or digging a spike so the ball can be fed to the star(s) with some consistency. Consequently, the most important part of volleyball is always to play cooperatively, in coordination with (and prepared to back up) teammates. The person playing the ball now should be thinking about the next person who will touch the ball, and that next person should be thinking about what to do to make it easier for the person now touching the ball.

2-on-2

Because the same person cannot touch the ball twice in a row in volleyball (other than a block, which does not count as a touch), a minimum of four people are necessary to play a game (2-on-2, or "doubles"). As shown in Figure 3-46, multiple starting positions and movements are possible even in doubles. Experienced partners work out which style and positioning works best for them. To ensure practice covering the court, it is helpful to set up a rule that the ball cannot be returned on the first hit.

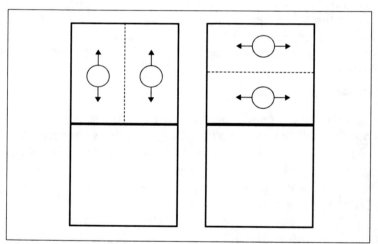

Figure 3-46. 2-on-2 starting positions and movements

In doubles, the order of ball contact is generally decided by who touched the ball first (player 1 passes, player 2 sets, player 1 attacks), and so players have to be moving constantly. This drill is ideal when trying to master the basic movements in volleyball. As in any version of volleyball, returning the ball by first-touch block/attack or second-touch attacks are relatively infrequent exceptions to the three touches allowed and used each time the ball crosses the net.

Basic—Points to Be Checked

- Players should always call out before passing the ball. This communication is especially important when a ball comes in between two players. Players should verbally indicate what they intend to do. Some coaches establish a rule that players should never call out "Yours" (to indicate they are not taking a ball) because they should always want the ball if they are in its vicinity, and calling out anything (other than a setter calling out "help" when he cannot reach a shanked pass) can be perceived as a call for the ball. Rather, passers should call out "Mine" (most of the time) or "Help" (infrequently) if they are in the vicinity of the ball (or are designated to take the ball under the applicable offensive system) but cannot reach it.
- The player who did not touch the ball first must always shift (usually opening his body to face the passer), prepare to receive the ball, and call out that he is ready (to give the passer a verbal cue where to pass the ball).

Advanced—Application

- It is not necessary to practice on a regulation volleyball court; a (smaller) badminton court will do just fine.
- Practicing on a smaller court necessitates more controlled actions (including less aggressive attacks). Consequently, smaller practice courts are especially helpful for teaching beginning players to use overhand and underhand passes. Smaller courts also promote longer rallies, which means more fun playing. If low skill level makes it difficult to maintain a rally of any length, change the rules to allow a single bounce.
- Suggestions for changing rules to fit skill levels (not all of which need apply simultaneously):
  - ✓ Direct that the ball must be returned on the third contact (touch) only. If it is returned on either the first or second touch/contact, it will not count.
  - ✓ Limit second contacts to overhand passes.
  - ✓ Require all contacts returning the ball to the opponent's court to include a jump (to spike, tip, etc.).
  - ✓ Allow a bounce during the volley.

3-on-3

At first glance, the only difference between doubles and 3-on-3 ("triples") would appear to be the addition of one more player per side. Surprisingly, that addition opens many more possibilities for positioning and strategy. Simply adding the option of passing to either one of the two non-passers reduces the need to force a pass to one player, allows more flexibility in the softness of a touch, and makes a variety of formations possible.

Starting Formations

Figure 3-47 illustrates some of the starting positions of each player before the opposing team sets the ball. Each of the many possible formations offers special characteristics.

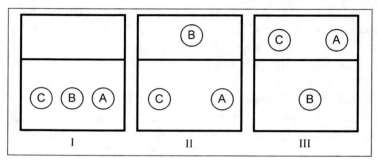

Figure 3-47. Starting positions for 3-on-3

Formation I

- In this formation, all three players are in a defensive position (0-3).
- This drill helps players learn to dig in their designated areas.
- Each player must learn or decide who is responsible to cover a particular area of the court during an opponent attack and must master the successive movements.

Formation II

- This formation shows one player blocking and two players prepared to pass (1-2).
- This drill helps establish and confirm the relationship between the block and the digging positions.
- B blocks all attacks, while the other players adjust their formation to the blocker's location (covering areas of the court the block does not cut off or protect). Thus, A and C shift to avoid being behind the blocker. They learn to play around the block.

Formation III

- In this formation, two players block, and one player passes or covers the court (2-1).
- This drill focuses on preparing the front row player not involved in a block to dig in the off-blocker role.
- If two players block together, the passer has more court to cover and often must hustle to the ball.
- Either A or C blocks, and the player who does not block prepares to dig. This drill replicates the movements the digger and off-blocker actually use in competition.

Adjusted Formations After Opponent Attacks From the Left

Figure 3-48 shows the 0-3 formation preparing for an attack from the left, with the players forming an arc facing the opponent attacker. In this formation, it is not necessary for the amount of space between the three players to be equal. Because the area covered by each player is different, the three players need to communicate and coordinate with each other. In the 1-2 formation, the two rear players should move to either side of the blocker. As in Figure 3-49, the rear players should not be in the zone behind the block; rather the rear players should move to the outside parts of the court to monitor the attack (and where the attacker is most likely to hit). In the 2-1 formation shown in Figure 3-50, front row player C, who does not jump for the block, should move back to the attack line, and take part in the passing/digging defense. If B can move rapidly enough, another possibility is to reproduce the 1-2 formation.

Figure 3-48. 0-3 adjusted formation after opponent attacks from the left

Figure 3-49. 1-2 adjusted formation after opponent attacks from the left

Figure 3-50. 2-1 adjusted formation after opponent attacks from the left

The defensive benefits of the 1-2 formation and the 2-1 formation will not be achievable if there is insufficient communication between the blocker(s) and the digger(s). For example, in the 1-2 formation, if the blocking player moves too far to the right, the area exposed to a cross attack increases. Similarly, in a 2-1 formation, if the players jump to block a cross attack, the opening for a spike straight down the line increases. In either case, a single defender's overreaction reduces the probability of a successful dig.

As soon as a ball has been dug, the passer and teammates should move into attack mode. First, the two players who did not dig should decide (if not predetermined) who should receive the pass (and therefore set), with the passer and remaining non-passer moving as quickly as possible to be able to hit the ball. It is critical for passers to call out to (or otherwise communicate with) each other to avoid mistaken assumptions that another player will pass the ball. Observation of the Gallaudet University volleyball team (or another team composed entirely of deaf players) is an education in superlative non-verbal communication on the court as well as team awareness and discipline of where each player is supposed to play and of what responsibilities he has for each play. Verbal communications are much easier to issue and receive.

Basic—Points to Be Checked

- After the first dig, one of the two players who did not dig must receive the pass and set the ball; otherwise, an attack will not happen. Players are more likely to make mistakes if they are not in synch with each other. Therefore, as in doubles, players must call out to each other as they play.
- As the number of players on the court increases (from doubles to triples up to the traditional six-player game), the movements required for blocking and digging correspondingly increase in importance. With almost inverse logic, the higher the number of players on the court, the more they rely on teammates fulfilling blocking

and passing responsibilities to decide where and how they will play; the fewer the players there are on the court, the more court each player expects to cover. Ideally, players should always compete with a doubles mentality (ready and willing to play, cover, or help everywhere) balanced by good communication with, and knowledge of, teammates to avoid interference and miscommunications.

Advanced—Application

- When a team cannot maintain a reasonably long rally in practice, establish rules to limit the attack locations (e.g., only back row attacks allowed) or types of attacks (e.g., no quick attacks allowed). These and similar adjustments make digging easier (improving passes and sets). Do not hesitate to be creative.
- Check the position of the setter. If the coach recommends that the setter receive passes in the A or B position in the 1-2 formation or the A position in the 2-1 formation, double-check the players' movements in these drills.
- Suggestions for changing rules to fit player skills:
  ✓ Mandate use of a three-stage attack, consisting of receive, set, and attack.
  ✓ Require the person who jumps to block to receive the pass and set.

4-on-4

A 4-on-4 game ("quads") is very similar to the full six-person game, as it requires players to practice the proper movements. With more players on the court, each player can block, determine how blocking affects defensive formations, and learn to coordinate with the setter.

Starting Formations

Figure 3-51 illustrates some of the starting positions of each player before the opposing team sets the ball. Each formation offers special characteristics or advantages. There are many other possible formations.

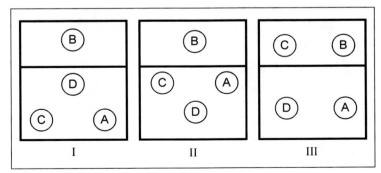

Figure 3-51. Starting positions for 4-on-4

Formation I: Triangle-and-One (Player Up)

- This formation employs a single blocker, one person in the center, and two players near the end line (1-1-2).
- D is in the ready position behind the blocker to receive a tip, and A and C cover the court areas not cut off by the blocker. It generally is assumed that a blocker will inhibit or block a spike straight at (or near) the blocker. This assumption suggests the only vulnerable area behind the blocker would be a dink or tip over the blocker (covered in this four-player formation), freeing the other two defenders to cover the areas not directly behind the blocker.

Formation II: Diamond (Player Back)

- Formation II involves a single blocker, two players in the center, and one person near the end line (1-2-1).
- B is responsible for trying to block all attacks, and the defensive formations are designed to complement the blocker's position.

Formation III: Box (Two Players Up)

- There are two blockers and two diggers in formation III (2-2).
- Generally, only B or C will block. The front row player who does not block should transition as quickly as possible into the defensive formation as a third digger.

Adjusted Formations After Opponent Attacks From the Left

In each formation, B jumps to block (Figures 3-52 through 3-54). Player D (in formation I), player A (in formation II), or player C (in formation III) moves and prepares to receive a tip. The diggers in the back have two patterns; in formations I and III, the players do not move, but in formation II, they shift. However, these patterns are not set in stone. In both formations I and III, the players need to make various decisions and then move. The constant challenge for the defense is determining the best formation to counter the particular offensive play. A, C, and D in the back must be in a ready position, playing around the blocker. Each such player must move to cover (defend against) the crosscourt attack or the line shot.

In 4-on-4, pick one player to be the setter and have him practice setting up attacks. Wherever possible, practice setting up combination attacks and have three different players, including the digger, touch the ball. For example, direct the player who blocks to approach for a high outside set, the player on the right side to do a pump attack, and the one on the left side a shoot attack. Usually, the setter should be in the tip reception position or the blocking position. Experiment with different patterns to determine which one(s) work best for a team.

Figure 3-52. Adjusted formation I after opponent attacks from the left

Figure 3-53. Adjusted formation II after opponent attacks from the left

Figure 3-54. Adjusted formation III after opponent attacks from the left

Basic—Points to Be Checked

- Use the regular rules.
- Pick a setter, and practice combination attacks. Practice passing to the setter's target area, and have the setter receive the pass.
- Coordinate blocking and digging.

Advanced—Application

- Use only tips and roll shots, and make sure each player moves properly.
- Decide on an attack pattern and order, and follow it (called a "scenario game" or game-situation practice).
- Use two balls, and play a game. Each team serves at the same time and keeps the balls going as long as possible. This drill develops player concentration with the simultaneous focus on frequent movements of the opposing team and of teammates.

4

Systems of Play

This chapter focuses on systems for playing the game of volleyball and explains how to develop or establish a system.

Progression of a System of Play

Given a ball and a group of people, chances are good the group will form a circle and start passing the ball back and forth. This is how volleyball starts. Everyone in a group passes a ball to someone else in the group while trying to avoid having the ball touch the ground. The atmosphere of such activity can be mildly intense as participants do not know when the ball will come to them. Other than making sure the ball does not touch the ground, no rules define who should do what or what should happen next. The more developed game of volleyball is played on a court partitioned by a net, involves an attack attempt within a span of only three contacts of the ball, defense and counter-attack by the opponent within three contacts (and possibly a block), with each team striving to score a point by having the opponent make a mistake or by causing the ball to touch the opponent's court. As a result, the pass-set-spike pattern was developed, and player roles became more specialized. In other words, a volleyball team plays in a space defined by the net, court boundaries, and allowable playing area (outside the court), with each competitor playing a specific role (or set of roles) in each rally. This pattern of integrated roles constitutes a team's playing system.

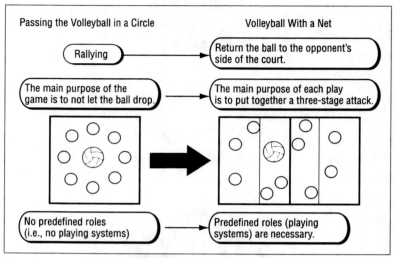

Figure 4-1. Evolution of volleyball

Figure 4-2 outlines the elements of a playing system. It can be divided into two main parts: team composition and playing systems.

Four basic types of playing systems are related to the player position, responsibilities, and movement required to respond to a situation during competition. Playing systems are classified by how the opposing team directs the ball across the net. These classifications are: serve receive system, attack receive system, free ball system, and block backup system. These four systems predefine each player's position and movement so the (counter) attack can proceed smoothly. The most important (frequently utilized) systems are the serve receive system and the attack receive system.

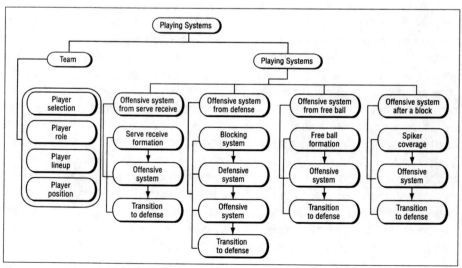

Figure 4-2. The playing system

Outside of rules defining where players may be in relation to teammates at the time of service and certain limitations on back row players in front of the three-meter line (the line on each half-court parallel to, and three meters from, the net), the types of formations and systems in volleyball are endless. Coaches should select those systems which best complement the skills and composition of their team. Review of some of the more common playing systems and their characteristics should help in making such decisions. Consider developing original formations using the explanations as a reference. Such decisions begin with methods for determining team composition.

Team Composition

Four elements relate to team composition. They are player lineup, player roles, player selection, and player positioning, as illustrated in Figure 4-3. Team composition strongly influences team tactics and team character.

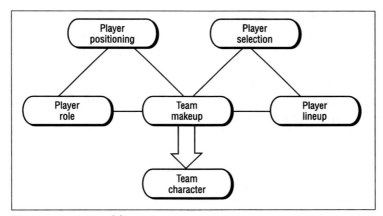

Figure 4-3. Assembling a team

Player Selection

As the term denotes, in the six-player system, only six players are permitted on each side of the court. The creation of the libero position (defensive specialist allowed unlimited back row entries for any player, prohibited from performing certain offensive actions, and distinguished from teammates by a different colored shirt) essentially gives teams seven starters. Therefore, choosing these starting players is very important. During a regular game, employing the rules applicable to six-player competition, each team may list 12 players on its roster (15 in USA Volleyball; 16 in NCAA), which means that up to 12 players can play in a game (set). Some teams have the starting players play the entire game, but it is more common to have other players substitute for one or more starters at times during the game. In assembling a team roster, coaches consider the combined strength and synergy of all 12 members.

An early question for coaches is whether to pick 12 players from which to select the starters or whether to pick the starters and then fill the roster with complementary substitutes (and/or players who could compete to become starters). To answer this question, player substitutions must be considered.

Up to six substitutions per game (set) are allowed internationally and 12 in USA Junior play and the collegiate game. However, there is a duality to all substitutions. In explanation, once player B substitutes for player A, player B cannot then substitute for any other player in that game. The most common approach with the (international) six-substitution rule is to have one to three pairs of player/substitute. In addition to the seven main members (including the libero), a team needs up to three quality substitute players, for a total of 10 players. These 10 people are the players who will be most active in a match and are, therefore, the most important. Thus, in assembling a team, these crucial 10 players are usually selected first, and then the remaining two players are chosen. Slight variations will be found in junior and collegiate play.

The creation of the libero changed the development and organization of team rosters and systems dramatically. Distinguished by a different colored team shirt as with goalies in soccer, the libero specializes in passing serves and digging spikes. Able to enter the game for any player without counting as a substitute, she can only play back row. It is illegal for a libero to direct a ball that is completely above the height of the net across the net from anywhere on the court (front or back row). The libero cannot set the ball with overhead finger action while any part of her body is touching the court on or in front of the three-meter line to a front *or* back row player, who then contacts the ball above the height of the net and directs it across the net. This position may not participate in a front row block even if she does not touch the ball. Internationally, the libero cannot serve. In USA college competition, the libero may serve in one position of the rotation.

The libero position was created in part to improve team defenses and lengthen rallies, and in part to design a position for which height was not an advantage (enable shorter players to compete at all levels of the game). As an ironic aside, top-level liberos have become so skilled that their precise and accurate passes enable setters to set plays and players with a higher probability of siding out (getting a kill) than before the libero position was created. Consequently, it has been argued that the libero position actually has shortened rallies overall.

A common use of liberos is to have them play back row for a team's two middle hitters, entering the game as soon as the middle hitter has sided out during her term of service. Middle hitters (often referred to as "middle blockers") tend to be a team's tallest players and, therefore, least able to "get low" and pass as well as teammates. Again, liberos can enter a game for any player and frequently will be used to enter or exit a game, creating a temporary pause with the goal of changing (interrupting) an adverse flow or sequence (in lieu of a timeout or substitution). Under the rules, a libero exchange (a libero entering or exiting for a player) is not supposed to slow the pace of a game; in reality, the officials will generally "give" the exchanging team an extra moment to complete the exchange.

The addition of the libero freed coaches to make more liberal use of substitutions for additional defensive skills, infuse fresh offensive or blocking strength, or rest a fatigued or frustrated setter. The FIVB is constantly experimenting with rules to extend rallies or otherwise make the game more exciting.

Player Roles

The location of players on the court (or position) and their function determine their roles.

Classification Based on Position

As illustrated in Figures 4-4 and 4-5, the three main positions are left, center, and right, which can be further separated into front row and back row. The position names most commonly used are shown in Figure 4-4. The numerical position system utilized by many countries is shown in Figure 4-5. As discussed in Chapter 1, positions are numbered starting with the server in the right back position (position 1), then moving to the right front position (position 2), i.e., the next server in the rotation, and so on.

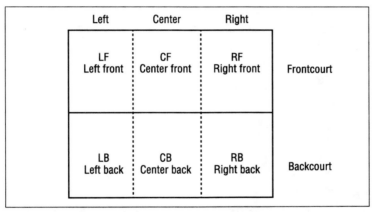

Figure 4-4. Most common position names

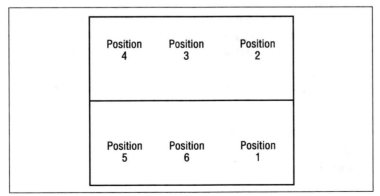

Figure 4-5. Position numbers

Classification Based on Player Functions

Players can be roughly separated into two groups, based on their functions: attackers and setters (Figure 4-6). In the six-player system, all players generally must be able to serve, receive, set, attack, and block. However, the basic breakdown of player functions includes classifying players by their specialty (e.g., attacking or setting).

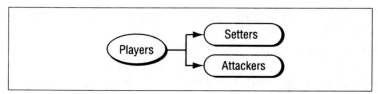

Figure 4-6. Types of players

Players can be further subdivided into the following categories:
- Defensive players: Players whose main role is defense.
- Offensive players: Players whose main role is offense.
- Blockers: Players whose main role is blocking.
- All-around players (universal players): Players expected to contribute to both offense and defense.
- Specialists:
    ✓ Attacking specialist (see Figure 4-7)
    ✓ Blocking specialists
    ✓ Defense specialists (including and especially the libero)

Assigning Roles

The ace (strongest or "strongside" hitter) usually plays on the left side. The strength of left side attack derives from the general strategy of having the setter face the left when setting, and most sets are front sets (toward the left where the setter can see) rather than (blind) back sets. However, nothing prevents a right side ("off side") player from being the ace or strongest hitter on a team. Indeed, remember that the right side hitter faces and blocks the left side ace of the opposing team. As athletic attackers often are superior blockers, coaches sometimes place their strongest all-round blocker/attacker on the right to counter the opponent's strongest attacker. In these situations, a team needs a setter able to deliver back sets accurately and consistently.

Assigning roles is accomplished by deciding positions and functions. Each individual's role should complement the team's needs for a particular match or situation. Figure 4-8 presents player roles cross-referencing positions with functions. Coaches should always take into account each player's individual specialties (and skills) when assigning roles.

Types of Attackers

Focus on the Point-Getters

Ace attacker: This player's role is to score and to get the serve for the team. Therefore, this player usually receives the most sets, and plays a central role in the team's offense. This player is the team's best attacker.

Assistant attacker: This attacker usually hits first or second tempo attacks. This player scores less than the ace attacker, but must be able to hit balls from various key points with a high degree of accuracy. This player is not as visible as the ace attacker, but plays a very important role on the team.

Super attacker: This position is fairly recent, only having been in use since 1994. This player must be able to hit a back row attack (i.e., jump and attack from behind the attack zone). This attacker is a pivotal offensive player, with a stronger image than the ace attacker, and is usually found in both the left and the right positions.

Focus on the Setting Tempo

Fast attacker: Usually does fast attacks and acts as a decoy for the tandem or crossing plays.

Second tempo attacker: Usually hits second tempo sets.

Slow attacker: Usually hits slow tempo sets.

Focus on the Skills of the Attacker

Power hitter: An attacker whose specialty is the height of the jump and the power of the hit.

Technical hitter: An attacker who can use various techniques, such as wipe-offs, tips, cut shots, pushes, and spot shots in an attack.

Figure 4-7. Types of attackers

Setter's Position

The setter usually delivers the set from the right or center front row (whether coming from the back row or playing front row). For a left (strong) side (generally right-handed) hitter, the easiest set to hit is from right. In other words, the setter should be on the right or the center so she can set a frontal, visible, easy-to-hit ball to the strongside attacker.

Back Positions

On most teams, the left, center, and right players only play one front line or back line position. Consequently, most teams will feature as starters two left side attackers, two middle blockers/attackers, one setter, and one right side attacker (often an attacker with

Function / Position	Setter	Attacker				
	Setter	Defensive	Offensive	All-Around (Universal)	Ace	Assistant
Left	Left setter	Defensive left	Offensive left	All-around left	Left ace	Assistant left
Center	Center setter	Defensive center	Offensive center	All-around center	Center ace	Assistant center
Right	Right setter	Defensive right	Offensive right	All-around right	Right ace	Assistant right

Figure 4-8. Example of player roles

backup setting skills) in addition to a defensive libero. Correspondingly, such starters generally play one back row position (if not replaced with a defensive specialist). Playing one front row or back row position means players will shift positions as soon as the ball is served.

By limiting the back line positions each individual plays, the players only need to practice one position. This specialization makes it possible to increase the technical competence and efficiency of practices. Beginning players should learn the basic skills of all positions. As they develop particular talents or physical attributes, it can be helpful to have them specialize in one or two positions. Moreover, even beginning or very young teams assign positions to players.

Position Changes

Once a coach has assigned positions to players, they must play in those positions for the offensive and defensive systems of the team to succeed. When a team is serving, the players should move to their positions as soon as the server contacts the ball (Figure 4-9). If a team is receiving the serve, players often move to their positions as soon as the ball is contacted for serve or once their team has attacked (Figure 4-10).

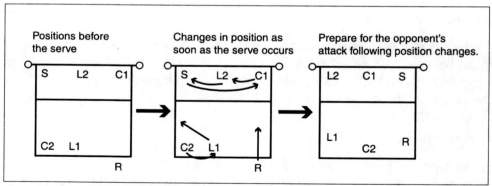

Figure 4-9. Examples of changing positions when serving

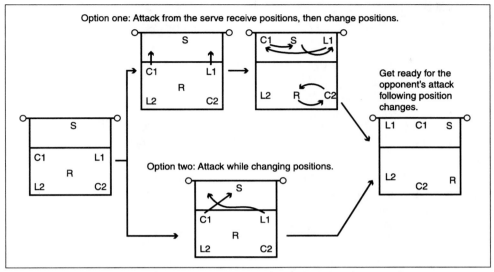

Figure 4-10. Examples of changing positions (when receiving the serve)

Player Lineup

The previous section examined the wide variety of player roles in volleyball. Another important element in assembling a volleyball team is having a balanced or cohesive selection of players to fulfill the different roles. This consideration is key in putting together the lineup for a game/set. The player lineup requires determination of how many players of each type to deploy and each player's role. The first decision is how many attackers and setters to deploy. As illustrated in Figure 4-11, there are 5-1, 6-2, and 4-2 offensive/setting systems. The first number of those systems represents the number of attackers, and the second is the number of setters.

The most common offensive system is the 5-1, or the one-setter system. In this system, the one setter sets, whether coming from the back row or while playing the front row. The big advantage of the 5-1 is that the attackers become accustomed to a

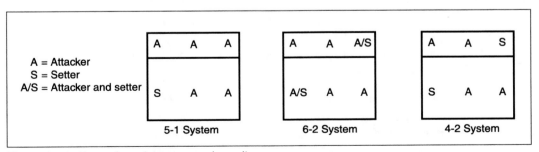

Figure 4-11. Examples of common player lineups

single style of setting. The potential disadvantages are the reduction to two attackers when the setter plays front row (countered in part by the potential for a setter surprise "dump" or attack on the second contact) and the greatly reduced playing time of (and, therefore, team familiarity with) the second or backup setter. In addition, the 5-1 system can be challenging when a team's primary setter is short and, therefore, a potential liability as a blocker.

In the 6-2, two-setter system, the two setters become attackers when they are in the front part of the court. This system has the advantages of maintaining three attackers in the front row and providing a second set of "hands" on the court. An alternative form of the 6-2 system has a team substitute for one or both setters when they rotate to the front row (a useful variation if either setter is a potential front row liability or significantly stronger offensive players are available to substitute). Similarly, the 4-2 is a two-setter system, but the two setters set primarily when playing the front row. This system makes the player lineup more defensive because there are only two front row attackers. The 4-2 is generally used by less experienced or beginning teams because a setter is always at or near the front row setting position to receive the pass.

Classifying Players in More Detail for Organizational Purposes

If a team had only defensive players, it would be very good at defense, but it would have minimal or no offensive abilities. In that situation, the team would score few points, and do so generally when the attacking team made a mistake. In parallel fashion, a team with only offensive players would have difficulty utilizing its strengths as its deficient defense would disable it from getting into a scoring position. Thus, it is essential for an offensive team to have an appropriate level of defensive skills and for a defensive team to have an appropriate level of offensive skills. In other words, it is necessary to deploy defensive players and offensive players in a well-balanced configuration. Teams tend to improve most when they train to improve their deficiencies (rather than focusing on improving their strengths) to reduce any imbalance between their offense and defense.

Correspondingly, coaches strive to reduce skill differentials among individual players to achieve a better balance between the strongest attackers and secondary attackers, first-tempo attackers and third-tempo attackers, and power hitters and technical hitters. Otherwise, opposing teams will concentrate on shutting down (defending against) a team's dominant attackers just as a well-prepared team will exploit an opponent's offensive or defensive weaknesses.

What exactly is a well-balanced team? It certainly does not mean having equal numbers of each type of player. In an extreme (and unlikely) example, if a team had five offensive players and only one defensive player with the defensive player being good enough to protect the other five players, the team would be well balanced. Balance is qualitative rather than quantitative.

Player Positioning

Player positioning refers to the locations of the six players in the first rotation (i.e., the starting lineup). Figures 4-12 through 4-14 have been provided as a reference to assist with deciding player positioning based on the skills, strengths, and weaknesses of a team.

5-1 System	6-2 System
L1: First left attacker	L1: First left attacker
L2: Second left attacker	L2: Second left attacker
C1: First center attacker	C1: First center attacker
C2: Second center attacker	C2: Second center attacker
R: Right attacker	SR1: Setter/First right attacker
S: Setter	SR2: Setter/Second right attacker

Figure 4-12. Player positions

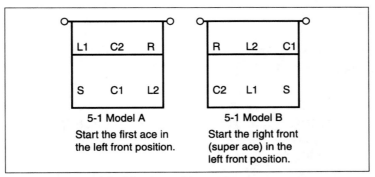

Figure 4-13. Model of basic positions of 5-1 systems

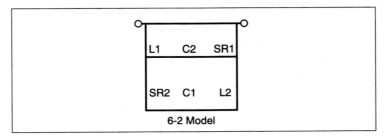

Figure 4-14. Model of basic positions of 6-2 systems

Principles of Player Positioning

- Place players with the same position and function (the two middle hitters, two left side attackers, two setters) diagonally (diagonal positioning principle) or opposite (three positions/rotations apart).
- An exception applies when playing in the 5-1 system (as there is no second setter), when the setter is positioned on the right and a right attacker is usually positioned diagonally from the setter. Very often, the right attacker opposite the setter is trained to receive the pass and serve as backup setter in situations when the setter is taken out of a play (e.g., when the setter passes or digs the ball).
- Correspondingly, there is only one libero. However, the libero is often used to replace two opposite players (such as the two middle hitters).
- The setter can also be positioned in the center but is not normally placed on the left. Note: Young, quick players with good hand-eye coordination who are left-handed are often encouraged to become setters. This encouragement occurs because setters tend to set from the front right or right-center, facing left with their left (attacking) arm away from the net (free to dump or attack the pass), and left-handed attackers hit more strongly from the right (whereas right-handed attackers hit more strongly from the left).
- To eliminate the weakest of the six rotations:
   ✓ When there are two ace attackers, place them diagonally from each other (Figure 4-15, left).
   ✓ When there are three point scorers working in different positions, position them in a triangle (Figure 4-15, right). The setter should be sandwiched between two of them.
- In the 5-1 system, the setter should be positioned in between a player who plays well with the setter (often a tall middle blocker who can "protect" a shorter setter and/or a middle who knows, likes, and is well able to hit a setter's especially quick sets) and the primary/stronger left attacker.
- Determine the starting lineup with the serve receive formation in mind. In model B-1, for example, L1 (the serve receiver), plays on the left twice and in the center once, but L2 plays once in the left, center, and right positions (Figure 4-16). This

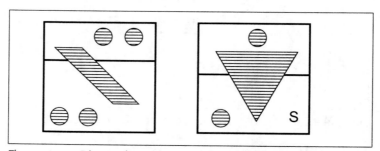

Figure 4-15. Diagonal positioning (left) and triangular positioning (right) of players

is the opposite of what happens in B-2 (Figure 4-17). Therefore, if L1 is good at receiving serves on the left, model B-1 is the best choice. If L1 can receive serves in any position and is good at setting up attacks, model B-2 is the better choice. This example illustrates the main point, which is that all players have an optimum receiving position. Keep this in mind when choosing a starting lineup.

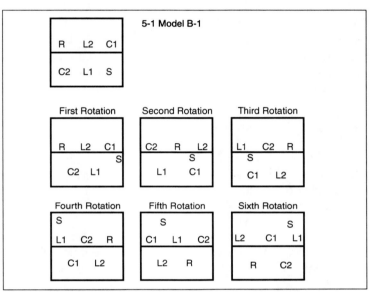

Figure 4-16. Model B-1 of the 5-1 system for the serve receive formation

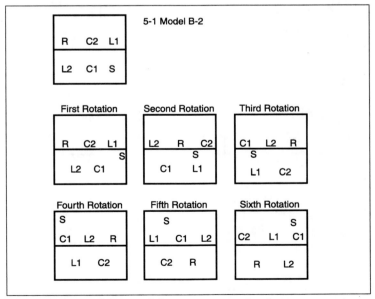

Figure 4-17. Model B-2 of the 5-1 system for the serve receive formation

Attacking From the Serve Receive

The ability to attack after the serve receive is essential in order to take the serve away from the opponent. If your team is not successful, the opposing team immediately scores a point. Consequently, it is important to design a serve receive formation that maximizes the aggregate passing strengths of a team's players and minimizes (or hides) its weaknesses. Minimizing passing errors, in turn, facilitates a counter-attack. The secondary goal of serve receive formation designs is to enable a team to transition most easily from serve receive to offense (secondary because a set and counter-attack are not possible without a successful serve receive/pass). To accomplish these goals, coaches must clearly understand each player's serve receive skills (and weaknesses) and his offensive abilities.

Traditional Serve Receive Formation

In the basic serve receive pattern, all players other than the setter receive serves. This formation is usually used when a team does not have a player who is adept at receiving serves. The area protected by each player is adjusted to match her level of ability. Figure 4-18 illustrates basic player positioning.

Establishment of the libero position essentially dedicated a player to act as a team's primary passer. The unlimited entries accorded a libero made it desirable to reserve a roster spot (or two) for a super defensive player. The limited number of substitutions previously

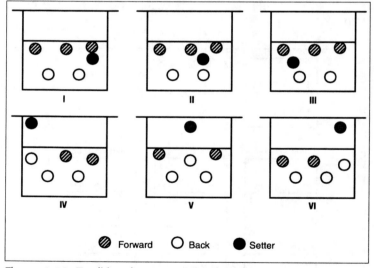

Figure 4-18. Traditional serve receive formation

allowed a defensive specialist caused many coaches to minimize pure defensive players who would have to leave the game upon rotation to the front row.

Positional Faults

Positional faults are closely related to the serve receive formation. Always consider the potential for positional faults when changing the formation for receiving a serve (through team confusion, lack of familiarity, or complexity). What, then, is a positional fault?

The rules of the game limit where players may be on the court in relation to each other at the moment the ball is contacted for serve. Once such contact takes place, players may move anywhere on the court, subject only to restrictions on actions by back row players on or in front of the attack line.

At the time of service, a back row player (e.g., left back/position 5) may be no closer to the net than the corresponding front row player (left front/position 4). Correspondingly, a front row player may be no closer to the end line than the corresponding back row player. Therefore, the front and back row players may be side by side. Further, a back row player may be closer to the net than a non-corresponding front row player (e.g., the left back player at position 5 may be closer to the net than the middle front at position 3 or right front player at position 2 and vice versa). The same types of limitations apply side to side with respect to players in the same row (front or back) as do the positional freedoms for players in different rows. These positional relationships are all based on player foot placements. Obviously, an infinite variety of formations are possible. Some coaches design formations to make front row players appear to be back row (or vice versa), especially early in a set to gain a potential surprise advantage over the as-yet-unaware opponent. These concepts are presented in Figure 4-19 for ease of understanding.

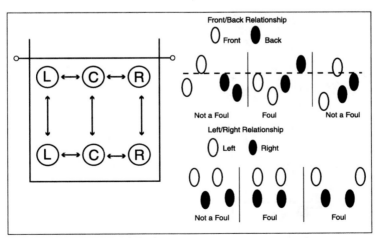

Figure 4-19. Positional faults

Changing Formations for Receiving Serves

Basic—Player Position Changes in the W Serve Receive Position (Figure 4-20)

Within each rotation, many potential variations are possible. The following points should assist coaches in determining the formation that best utilizes a team's abilities:

- It is easier for the setter to play alongside the net. Even an agile setter should be placed in a position from where it is easy to set (to improve setting).
- The player who is best at receiving a serve should be placed in the center of the court to maximize the probability of that player receiving the ball.
- Consider the opponent's weak points. For example, if the opposing team is especially vulnerable to a team's left side attacker, variation (b) in Figure 4-20 is better than (c), as the primary attacker would be in a position to receive more sets early in the game (set).

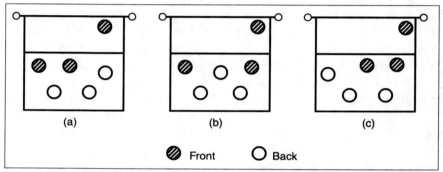

Figure 4-20. Player position changes in the W serve receive position (basic)

Advanced—Changes to the Serve Receive Formation

- Diagonal W formation (Figure 4-21)

This formation places the setter close to where the pass should arrive (making it easier for the setter to set) and facilitates quick attacks.

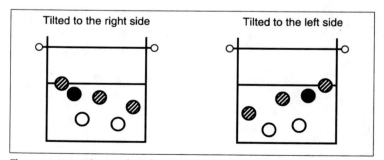

Figure 4-21. Diagonal W formations

• Advanced—Upside-down W formation (Figure 4-22)

With three players positioned in the back row (making an upside-down W), this formation can be good for receiving an unusually difficult jump serve. A jump serve's trajectory is low and fast, and the ball usually drops near the base line, making it difficult for only two players to handle; adding a third receiver to the area where the ball likely will drop reduces the reaction distance needed to reach the ball, improving the chances of a good pass.

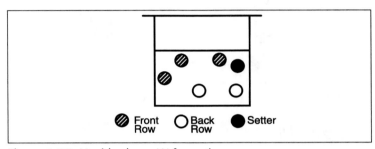

Figure 4-22. Upside-down W formation

• Advanced—Four-player formation (Figures 4-23 and 4-24)

By shielding or hiding a weaker passer, this formation maximizes the probability of a stronger passer receiving serve. This formation also makes it easy for a quick attacker to get into position for a first-tempo attack.

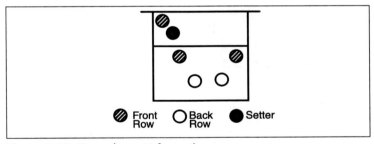

Figure 4-23. Four-player U formation

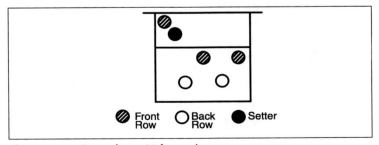

Figure 4-24. Four-player N formation

- Advanced—Three-player formation (Figure 4-25)

This formation makes use of players who specialize in receiving serves, hitting quick attacks, or hitting back row attacks.

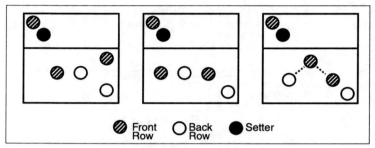

Figure 4-25. Three-player formation (advanced)

- Advanced—Two-player formations (Figure 4-26)

Like the three-player formation, the two-player formation makes use of players who specialize in receiving serves, hitting quick attacks, or hitting back row attacks.

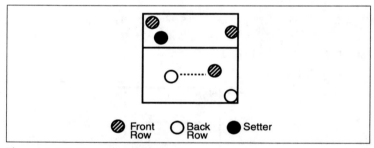

Figure 4-26. Two-player formation

Deciding on Attack Patterns

The types of attacks executed by individual players were explained previously. This section examines offensive patterns for the whole team.

In designing combination attacks, the defining characteristic is moving all attackers into attack position so even non-attacking players can act as decoys. Many higher level combination attacks include back row attacks. A common version of this offensive strategy calls for the front row attackers to gather in the left and center positions and for the back row attacker to hit a second-tempo attack from the right. This attack uses the front row attackers as decoys.

The examples that follow describe just a few of the possible combination attacks, but they show how to put together unique attack patterns, taking advantages of attackers' strengths.

- Basic—Straight (Figure 4-27)
- Basic—Straight with a first tempo (using the width of the court) (Figure 4-28)
- Basic—Tandem (first and second tempo) (Figure 4-29)
- Basic—Straight (first tempo C quick) (Figure 4-30)
- Basic—Cross (right side X) (Figure 4-31). The center front moves to make an A quick attack, and the right front moves to make the second-tempo attack in the front two position.
- Basic—Cross (left side X) (Figure 4-32). The center front moves to make a B quick attack, and the left front moves to the second-tempo attack in the front two position.
- Advanced—Double quick (first tempo with a left and right front, middle swings) (Figure 4-33)
- Advanced—Double quick (first tempo with a left and middle front, right side X) (Figure 4-34)
- Advanced—Tandem (right side swing) (Figure 4-35)
- Advanced—Double quick (right side swing) (Figure 4-36)
- Advanced—Middle swing and backcourt attack (Figure 4-37)
- Advanced—Back slide and backcourt attack (Figure 4-38)

Figure 4-27. Straight

Figure 4-28. Straight with a first tempo

Figure 4-29. Tandem

Figure 4-30. Straight (first tempo C quick)

Figure 4-31. Cross (right side X)

Figure 4-32. Cross (left side X)

Figure 4-33. Double quick attack (1)

Figure 4-34. Double quick attack (2)

Figure 4-35. Tandem and swing

Figure 4-36. Double quick and swing

Figure 4-37. Middle swing and backcourt attack

Figure 4-38. Back slide and backcourt attack

Practice Points and Drills

Practice Points:

- Design combination attacks to make the attackers' movements flow more smoothly and to avoid confusion and collisions.
- Emphasize the need to call out who will receive the serve as quickly as possible and make sure that passers maintain a clear view of the server. Coaches have learned to group serving team players to hide or obscure views of the server. At the highest competitive levels, such screening has become blatant and almost universal. Coaches of receiving teams should not hesitate to instruct their captains to ask referees to watch for and address screens, especially with younger players.

- Confirm the movements needed to provide cover (safety plays, secondary setters, shoot passes to distant corners when a set/spike is impossible) when serve reception becomes disorganized. Confirm who will set on the second hit when the primary setter is taken out of a play, either because she was the passer or the pass was so far from target the setter could not reach it.

Basic—Free Serve

Have a player serve underhanded from about three meters ahead of the base line of the opponent's court to practice setting up combination attacks from superior passes (of free balls or easy serves). Repeat the drill as necessary to develop smooth player movement as attackers move to attack and other players transition to support positions. Some teams have a coded ("1," "2," or "3") set of more complicated attacks (often combination attacks) when a free ball (easy, high, looping return) or easy serve is identified (creating the expectation of a good or excellent pass). Even free balls or easy serves can be incorrectly passed, so these complicated attacks usually have an outlet— an attacker who could be given an easy, high set from a poor pass.

Advanced—Bench Serve

Have someone standing on a bench behind the end line hit a strong serve and develop contingency plans for movements and outlet plays when the serve receive cannot be correctly returned to the setter.

Attacking After Receiving an Attack or Playing Defense

Improving Blocking Skills

To improve a team's ability to handle an opponent's offensive plays, the first thought most often is to improve the digging skills of each player. Such narrow focus risks abject failure to achieve the goal of successfully digging the (majority of the) wide range of offensive plays common in modern volleyball. To achieve such a goal, it is necessary to coordinate effective blocking with digging. In other words, a team's digging formation should be based upon its blocking pattern. With minor variables, the blocking pattern, in turn, evolves with an opponent's offensive play. In general, teams use a block at the point of attack to keep the ball from going into certain areas of the court and deploy the remaining players to the other parts of the court (not protected by the block), prepared to dig. As a result, backcourt digging poorly coordinated with the block will be erratic as no clear plan will be in place to "cover" or defend the entire court (via blocker or passer/digger).

It is instructive to review jumping patterns for blocks, using a model where two players block an attack from the left. Figure 4-39 (I) illustrates the basic jumping pattern, where two players equally block a ball (i.e., the ball is centrally located between their two sets of hands). Figure 4-39 (II) illustrates a slight shift of the block to the right to cut off a crosscourt spike. The players jump so the outside player is the primary blocker. Figure 4-39 (III) illustrates a shift of the block to the left to cut off a spike down the side line. The players jump so the inside player becomes the primary blocker. In each case, it is necessary to match the block to the opponent's attack. In other words, certain attackers have a tendency to hit cross court or down the line. Coaches often adjust to counter an opponent's strengths or tendencies.

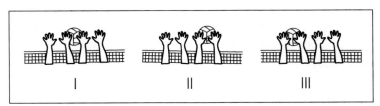

Figure 4-39. Basic jumping pattern

In turn, diggers are positioned (or shifted) on the court based on the location of the blockers. Figure 4-40 illustrates a crosscourt spike from the left. It is almost impossible for a digger positioned behind the blocker (as shown on the right side of Figure 4-40) to dig the ball because the blocker obstructs the digger's view of the ball, and the blocker is the first line of defense as the attacker will endeavor to hit the ball to "open" court (court not shut off by the blockers or defended by diggers). Diggers should always be in a ready position where they can see the ball (as shown on the left side of Figure 4-40). Teams should practice predicting or reading an opponent's attack (based on factors such as the opponent's pass, set, and individual strengths and tendencies) and then coordinate the block and defense (ensuring diggers can always see the ball).

Figure 4-40. Crosscourt spike from the left

Attack Receive of Defensive Formations and Characteristics

Review of three common game situations helps illuminate the necessity of different types of defensive formations. One situation occurs when the setter receives the ball, because there is a possibility the setter will attack on the second hit; another situation is when an opponent spikes the ball; a third situation is when the attack is actually received. In each situation, the formation adjusts in response to the opposing team's plays. Formations do not have a single set of positions but, rather, are fluid and constantly changing.

- Situation 1: The opponent's setter touches the ball (the initial formation or base position).
- Situation 2: The opposing attacker hits the ball (the home position or read, release, and adjusted position).
- Situation 3: The ball is received (the pursuit point).

The Initial Formation or Base Position

The initial formation is needed in case the setter attacks on the second of the three available touches of the ball, or in case the setter sets a quick attack. In these situations, it is helpful to position players near the attack line in one of two typical formations. Figure 4-41 depicts the player-back formation that places two players on either sideline, and Figure 4-42 depicts the player-up formation, which places one player in the center of the court. The dotted lines identify the formations' weak points. When facing an opponent who often targets the sides of the court, a team using the player-up formation would be at a disadvantage and would have to find a way to counter its vulnerabilities. This can be done by allowing one player to move freely, slightly changing the formation, or by changing the blocking pattern.

From here on, descriptions of formations will be based on the initial formation or base position. Player locations will be expressed in the following order: the number of players near the net, the number of players on the attack line, and the number of players on the baseline. Figure 4-42 would be expressed as a 3-1-2 formation.

Figure 4-41. Player-back formation

Figure 4-42. Player-up formation

The Release and Adjusted Positions

For defense against an attack from the left or right, the initial formations shown in Figures 4-41 and 4-42 are adjusted as illustrated in Figures 4-43 through 4-46. In option 1, player 1 is poised to receive a tip from the left (Figure 4-43); in option 2, it is player 6 who is ready to receive a tip from either the left (Figure 4-44) or right (Figure 4-46). In option 1, for defense from either the left (Figure 4-43) or right (Figure 4-45), player 6 is positioned to receive a line spike or a ball hit to the baseline, while in option 2 this role is taken over by player 1 for defense from the left (Figure 4-44)

Figure 4-43. Formation for defense from the left (option 1)

Figure 4-44. Formation for defense from the left (option 2)

and player 5 for defense from the right (Figure 4-46). In both options, players 4 and 5 are positioned to cover a crosscourt spike for defense from the left (Figures 4-43 and 4-44) and players 1 and 2 are positioned to cover a crosscourt spike for defense from the right (Figures 4-45 and 4-46).

To reach the release position from the initial formation or base position, players need to move during the brief period between the set and the attack. When compared with Figures 4-41 and 4-42 showing the two initial formations, it is clear that in option 1, players 4, 5, and 6 and players 1, 2, and 6 must move to reach the positions in Figures 4-43 and 4-45, respectively. To reach the positions in option 2 (Figures 4-44 and 4-46), only players 4 and 6 and players 2 and 6, respectively, need move to complete the formation. Therefore, slower teams should use the formation shown in Figures 4-44 and 4-46. Remember that the weak points illustrated/inherent in the initial formation become more pronounced in the home position.

Figure 4-45. Formation for defense from the right (option 1)

Figure 4-46. Formation for defense from the right (option 2)

Figures 4-47 and 4-48 illustrate formations using a single blocker in response to an attack from the center. To utilize two blockers, either player 2 or 4 must move up to block beside player 3. Such formations, however, would leave a space where they had been available to play a passing defense, and it will be necessary to cover (have another player take responsibility for balls hit to) this space. In Figure 4-47, either player 2 or 4 can dig a tip, while in Figure 4-48, it is player 6's responsibility. However, in the formation depicted in Figure 4-47, there is a high possibility that players 2 and 4 might expect the other to dig the tip, and neither will move to dig it. Therefore, it is necessary to assign the reception area for each player carefully.

To transition into the formation in Figure 4-47 from the initial formation, players 2 and 4 do not block, but rather move back slightly, as do players 1 and 5. Therefore, the shape of the initial formation is preserved when responding to an attack from the center; so, too, though, are the vulnerabilities designated by the dotted lines. The formations shown here are only examples. Every team should modify formations to counter an opponent's strengths (and exploit its weaknesses).

Figure 4-47. Formation using a single blocker in response to an attack from the center (option 1)

Figure 4-48. Formation using a single blocker in response to an attack from the center (option 2)

The Pursuit Point or React Phase

In this position, players actually dig the ball. Because the amount of time between a spike and the dig or pass is so short, players rarely shift out of the release position. However, in cases where there is more time to react, such as when a block deflects an attack, the formation might change drastically. Quick judgment and agile movement are vital in digging. The measure of a digger is how well she can move to and pass a ball in the area one to three meters around her ready position.

Transitioning to Offense

Attack patterns differ depending on how the ball is handled after reception. Better passes create more options for the setter; conversely, poor passes reduce the attacking options. Therefore, it is necessary to practice responses to the three situations described in Figure 4-49 for each rotation of the six players. The location of the set and the attack pattern will change, depending on whether the setter is in the front or back line. It is vital to consider these variables and create predetermined responses to each situation that all six players on the court understand and implement.

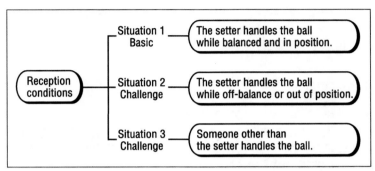

Figure 4-49. Reception conditions

Situation 1 offers the widest variety and most successful offensive plays. In this situation, the ball is passed to the area ahead of the attack line, near the center of the net. No team passes perfectly every time. It is vital, therefore, to consider multiple variations and conditions, such as the setter's location upon digging and her speed. It is also important that the attackers be prepared for a set any time the ball has been passed to the setter. The front line players should practice shifting rapidly from blocking and reception positions to attack position.

In Situation 2, the setter receives the pass in a difficult or awkward position. In this situation, the setter's options are usually limited to slower and/or higher front row sets. Consequently, each of the front attackers must be ready to attack. As any pre-planned play must change with a poor pass, it is necessary to call out the location and the height of the set as soon as possible, to alert the attackers of the change in play. Many teams assign a code to the alternative play, whether a number, color, or something else.

Situation 3 occurs when a passer severely shanks the ball out of the setter's reach or when the setter makes the first contact with the ball after it crosses the net. In most cases, the resulting set on the second hit or touch will be of inferior quality, undermining the quality or strength of the resulting attack.

Both the front line players and the back line players should be prepared to participate in the play. The player who sets the ball should visually verify where she intends to set the ball and verbally alert or cue the attackers as soon as possible. When the setter makes the first contact, she must decide whether to set the ball immediately or to pass it to the player on the right and shift into position to attack. Many teams have a pre-identified secondary setter to whom these default passes are directed, when possible.

Practice Points and Drills

Practice Points:

- Practice so receivers do not take up position directly behind the blocker(s).
- Practice shifting into an attack pattern after a bad reception.
- Practice attacking after the first hit (touch), in case the receiver does not pass the ball to the setter.

Basic—Tabletop Reception

Have a player serve (difficult or challenging) balls into the court while standing on a table and practice putting together attacks after receiving/passing the ball. Carefully practice one formation at a time (repetitively) to ensure that the players clearly understand the transition from receiving to attacking.

Advanced—Combination Attack

Practice combination attacks following a poor pass. The attackers should move from their blocking or receiving position to a spiking position. Design the drill so it mirrors game situations as much as possible.

Advanced—Second Hit Attacks

Practice attacking on the second hit for every rotational variation. Conduct this drill while clarifying who will set the ball when it is passed to different areas of the court. Attackers should consider responses to different scenarios during practice (for example, a tandem attack or a strong baseline hit).

Free Ball Attacks

Decide on several patterns for attacking after receiving a free ball. A free ball occurs when the return by the opposing team can be easily controlled (such as a high looping ball over the net, saving a shanked pass). The expectation is that the pass of a free (easy) ball has a very high probability of accuracy, thereby giving the setter more options and time to choose the attacker who can (and type of attack which will) challenge the defense.

The shift to the free ball formation, which is different from the attack receive formation, begins when it is determined that the opponent's attack can be easily received. Teams should predetermine (in practice) who will identify free balls. Generally, this role falls to the center blocker, who decides whether to jump, or to the setter, who organizes the plays. To ensure a team works in unison, it is imperative the team members on the court know who will make the decision and how the decision will be signaled. If the players do not move in a predetermined manner, holes will open in their defense, they will make mistakes, and/or the opponent will score.

Types of Free Ball Formations and Attacks

The free ball formations are illustrated in this section using the 3-2-1 and 3-1-2 initial formations. Figures 4-50 and 4-51 illustrate formations where the setter is in the front. Once a free ball has been identified, the front line players move to the attack line and prepare to attack, while the back line players move to predetermined positions to receive the ball.

Figure 4-50. 3-2-1 pattern (setter in front)

Figure 4-51. 3-1-2 pattern (setter in front)

Figures 4-52 and 4-53 illustrate formations in which the setter is in the back. Passing patterns change to allow back line setters time to get into position. Back row setters especially must do their best to give the free ball signal quickly to inform receivers where to pass the ball as they hasten to where they expect to receive the free ball pass. To increase the possibility of an effective attack, the free ball receiver should be one of the back line players who are not involved in the attack. Preparations for the attack will be impeded if one of the attacking players receives.

Figure 4-52. 3-2-1 pattern (setter in back)

Figure 4-53. 3-1-2 pattern (setter in back)

Again, the setter (or other designated player) should give the free ball signal as soon as possible and set up the appropriate combination attack. Advanced teams sometimes practice quick passes to setters on free balls because of the increased probability of an accurate pass and to try to mount an attack before the defense is prepared to receive.

Practice Points and Drills

Practice Points:

- Practice moving to the free ball formation.
- Practice controlling the ball in response to the setter's signal.
- Practice attack patterns where the setter makes the first contact with the ball.

Basic—Free Ball Formation

Put the ball in play in a simulated free ball and confirm that the players consistently know where to go for the free ball formation. Modify the drill to expose players to the variety of ways in which the ball can enter the court (see Figure 4-54) and to meet (and challenge) the players' skill levels.

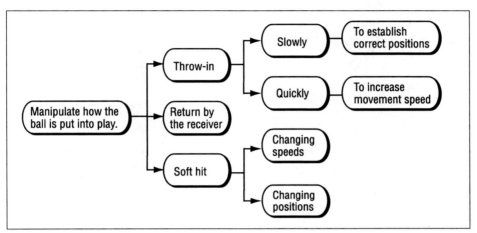

Figure 4-54. Ways in which a free ball may enter the court

Basic—Attacking After the Setter Makes First Contact With the Ball

Put the ball in play so the setter receives it (first contact), and then confirm the appropriate attack formation. Control of free balls should be much easier than when receiving an attack, so practice putting together combination attack plays. It should be a relatively rare occurrence for the setter to receive a free ball. As soon as a ball has been identified as free, everyone on the team should know the setter will be moving to her front row setting position prepared to receive a precise and/or quick pass from which to develop a more aggressive or deceptive attack reserved for free balls. This foreknowledge should cause the reception pattern to adjust so non-setters will cover the setter's receiving position. Nonetheless, players need to know what to do and where to move when the setter receives the first ball. Note that one option is for setters to set a free ball for a second touch attack.

Attacking After Saving a Blocked Attack

Attacking after saving a blocked ball is much less common than other types of offense because players are not in their receive, set, and attacker positions when the blocked ball is dug or saved. Many teams do not even practice setting up an attack following the recovery of a blocked ball. However, being able to convert a blocked ball into an effective offensive play can change the way a game unfolds. Moreover, it is important that players be ready to make a save when a teammate attempts an attack (covering the attacker). Practice transitioning from receive to set, and to covering the attacker to whom the set has been directed.

It is just as important to practice attack coverage formations as the more common plays. Practicing coverage drills enhances a team's ability to respond automatically to most game situations.

Formations and Attacks After a Block Is Saved

Most attacks occur on the left. Accordingly, this section begins with methods for saving a blocked attack on this side.

The Positions for Saving a Blocked Attack

- Basic—2-3 Spiker Coverage Pattern (Figure 4-55): Two players line up in a row immediately behind the attacker; behind them is a row of three players.
- Basic—3-2 Spiker Coverage Pattern (Figure 4-56): Three players line up in a row immediately behind the attacker; behind them is a row of two players.

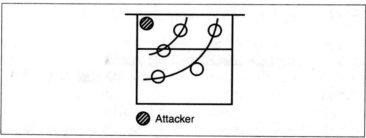

Figure 4-55. 2-3 spiker coverage pattern (basic)

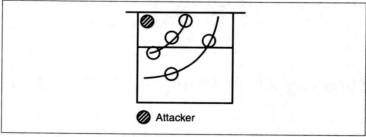

Figure 4-56. 3-2 spiker coverage pattern (basic)

Moving Into Spiker Coverage Positions From Serve Receive Formations

- Basic—W Formation
  - ✓ When there is no quick attack (Figures 4-57 and 4-58)
  - ✓ When there is a quick attack (Figures 4-59 and 4-60)
- Advanced—Four-Person Serve Receive Formation (U Formation) (Figure 4-61)
- Advanced—Four-Person Serve Receive Formation (N Formation) (Figure 4-62)

Figure 4-57. Moving into spiker coverage positions from W formation—attack from the left

Figure 4-58. Moving into spiker coverage positions from W formation—attack from the center

Figure 4-59. Moving into spiker coverage positions from W formation—quick attack from the left

Figure 4-60. Moving into spiker coverage positions from W formation—quick attack from the center

Figure 4-61. Moving into spiker coverage positions from U formation

Figure 4-62. Moving into spiker coverage positions from N formation

Practice Points and Drills

Practice Points:

- Practice setting up formations in which players do not cover the same area.
- Practice these formations in combination attacks (when the player who hits a quick attack does not move to save).
- Identify and reinforce where saved blocks should be passed and the player movements after a controllable ball has been saved.

Basic—Rebounding (Figure 4-63)

In this three-person drill, have an attacker intentionally hit the ball into a blocker while two other players, one who set the ball and one positioned to cover the spiker, attempt to save the blocked attack. If the ball is saved, set the ball, and repeat the drill continuously.

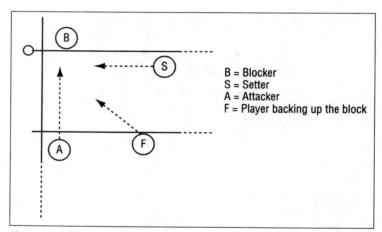

B = Blocker
S = Setter
A = Attacker
F = Player backing up the block

Figure 4-63. Rebounding

Advanced—Six-Person Blocking

Practice with two people in the left, center, and right positions on the opponent's side of the court (six blockers) to increase the probability of a blocked attack. Serve from the opponent's side to a regular six-person serve receive formation. Have the receiving team concentrate on accurate passes (always a primary goal), developing a combination attack, covering the attackers (blocked attack save formation), and transitioning from a saved block to another combination attack. Instruct the serving team to (try to) put three blockers on each attack so the attacking side will be able to practice game situation recoveries or saves of blocked attacks.

5

Coaching Guide

Previous chapters examined the skills and systems necessary to play volleyball. This chapter focuses on methods for teaching volleyball skills and systems and on developing and organizing effective volleyball drills.

Understanding the Skills, Tactics, and Strategies of Volleyball

Skill, system, tactics, and strategy are important components of a volleyball match. An understanding of these concepts (or failure to understand any of them) significantly impacts an individual player's rate of improvement and ability to apply skills in team play. Players must understand the concepts behind skills, systems, tactics, and strategy, as well as their interrelationship, to improve both personal skills and the ability of the team as a whole.

However, it is difficult to define the concepts behind skill, system, tactics, and strategy. In the book *Abriß einer Theorie der Sportspiele*, H. Döbler states that tactics in ball sports are "the total procedures taken individually and as a team, offensively and defensively, based on considerations of how to proceed against opponents in order to achieve the best possible outcome" (Döbler, 242).

Tactics are also called "the logic behind the methods of leading an individual or team, and adapting them to different methods of competition (methods of offense and defense)" (Itagaki, 31). It is clear that tactics are the logic that influence how a team plans, acts, and reacts to compete against an opponent. It nonetheless can be difficult for coaches to understand the interrelations of the team actions and reactions which define tactics.

This chapter will endeavor to introduce basic tactics. The explanations for each tactic include supplementary information to facilitate understanding.

As can be seen from Figure 5-1, the elements of volleyball coaching (excluding indirect factors such as recruiting) consist of three factors (systems, tactics, and strategy), which are supported by individual skill. Begin by looking at systems.

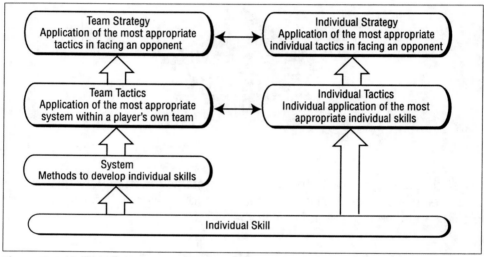

Figure 5-1. Volleyball strategy and tactics system

System

System generally refers to methods that enable players to use their skills on the court. Play systems in volleyball include the locations and the movements of players during competition.

Tactics

Team-specific tactics refer to the application or adjustment of a system to take full advantage of each player's abilities. Tactics must match the players' individual technical abilities. In other words, if a player cannot execute a jump set well or effectively, it would be fruitless to use tactics that call for a player to fake spiking the ball and then perform a jump set. Tactics also include using a system to hide or protect players' weak points and take full advantage of their strengths. In other words, play systems are options through which tactics can be developed. When a coach employs a system to take full advantage of a team's ability, that play system becomes the team's tactic.

Strategy

Strategy refers to the identification and application of the tactics that would work most successfully against a particular opponent (i.e., selecting tactics that are most likely to defeat an opponent). In one sense, because of player rotation in six-player volleyball, an opponent is actually six opponents. Because the front line and back line players change with each rotation, so should the play system. Therefore, when considering strategy, coaches must consider not just one strategy, but, rather, six strategies to counter each rotation of the opponent. The most appropriate strategy for each rotation is known as its "matchup."

Correlation With Individual Skill

The previous concepts focused on the team as a whole, but team tactics are only a single aspect of the sport. Coaches also must consider individual tactics. In the previous definition for tactics, replacing the word system with the phrase "individual skill" defines individual tactics. Individual tactics refer to the application of specific individual skills to optimize or maximize a player's overall performance or contribution to the team's success. For example, an attacker who spikes weakly or does not jump very high could be taught or instructed to fake a hit to wipe off the block, fake a hit to draw a block, tip, or shoot the ball to a distant corner. Such a strategy would mask the player's weak points and enable the player to make a positive offensive contribution to the team. In corollary fashion, "individual strategy" is the selection and application of tactics to counter a specific opponent's strengths and exploit its weaknesses or vulnerabilities. Individual skills are the foundation of individual tactics and individual strategy, as well as team tactics and team strategy.

Ballhandling

As shown in Figure 5-2, it is necessary to develop individual skill, a play system, and ballhandling to design tactics and strategy. Although often forgotten, ballhandling is *the* vital factor that enables and dictates tactics. Space (passing locations), speed, rotation, and trajectory are the elements (and variables) of ballhandling.

Variations in ballhandling will cause changes in play style, even if the play system is identical. For example, a pass to the setter with a low trajectory will increase the tempo of play as players rush to be in place when the setter receives the ball. It is not enough just to pass; players must consider how the characteristics of their pass will affect play.

Conducting Practices

Before discussing how to conduct practices, it is important to emphasize the importance of the fundamentals and application of individual skills. Fundamental skills

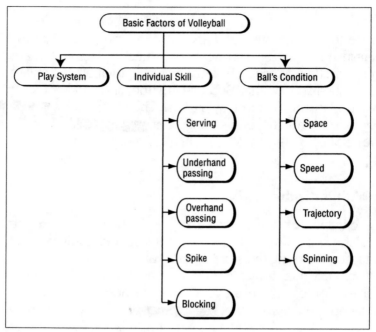

Figure 5-2. Volleyball tactical structure

and their applications are also essential aspects of group and team play. The skill levels of individual play, group play, and team play all affect the outcome of a game. Players need not completely master every volleyball skill to play because the sport can be enjoyed by beginners and advanced players alike. Nonetheless, by conducting practice appropriately, it is possible to strengthen a team and improve the skills of its individual players. The progression outlined in the following sections is designed for the long term (over the course of a year or more), but can be modified to apply to a single practice.

First, Strengthen Team Play

A game consists of two teams competing against each other, so a team must be (trained and) able to react to an opponent's plays. Many skills must be acquired to make this possible.

As shown in Figure 5-3, each player must first acquire the five fundamental volleyball skills (serving, passing, setting, spiking, and blocking). Next, the team members must learn how to work together to implement coordinated plays. In the early stages of team development, it is premature to focus on the opponent. The skills (and knowledge) of measuring, planning for, and reacting to opponents naturally follow the development and refinement of individual and team skills. This sequence suggests the most logical progression for practicing.

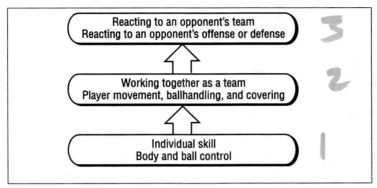

Figure 5-3. Ideal progression for practices: Individual skills →
teamwork → scrimmages

The Relationship Between Individual Skill and Group Skill

Figure 5-4 depicts the basic pattern of refining individual skills and then group and team skills. As individual and team skills improve, the pattern is repeated, steadily improving the team's skill level.

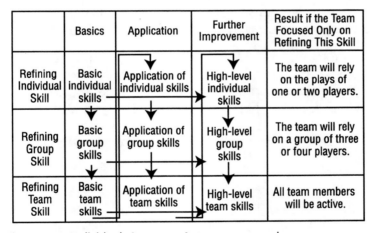

	Basics	Application	Further Improvement	Result if the Team Focused Only on Refining This Skill
Refining Individual Skill	Basic individual skills	Application of individual skills	High-level individual skills	The team will rely on the plays of one or two players.
Refining Group Skill	Basic group skills	Application of group skills	High-level group skills	The team will rely on a group of three or four players.
Refining Team Skill	Basic team skills	Application of team skills	High-level team skills	All team members will be active.

Figure 5-4. Individual → group → team progression

It is possible to accelerate development of an individual player's skills by focusing on only those skills in practice. Such narrow focus, however, ignores and inhibits improvement of overall team performance. In such situations, teams become overly dependent on the play of one or two players. As emphasized throughout this book, volleyball is the ultimate team game. Once served, a ball cannot come to rest or be touched twice by the same player (except in the unique case of a block) without losing the point. Similarly, by focusing practice on three- or four-player group drills, the team will come to rely primarily on those three or four players. By practicing to improve individual skills, group skills, and team skills through balanced practices and drills along with game situation drills utilizing six players on a side, a team's performance level will improve and the team will make the best use of all the players' skills.

Skill Levels and Practice Objectives

Practices must reflect the skill level of the team (sufficiently difficult to challenge but not so difficult as to demoralize or be impossible to complete). As a team's skill level increases, practices must similarly evolve.

Figure 5-5 displays skill levels, aspects of the game appropriate for practice at each skill level, and rules that can be used in practice games to help develop the desired skills. The five levels of skill are outlined, starting with a player's introduction to volleyball. At each level, the focus should be on obtaining and refining the skills that define that level (these skills are listed in the "Goals" boxes in Figure 5-5). By watching and judging a team's play, coaches should determine goals appropriate for the team (and each player on that team) and plan practices accordingly.

Remember that skill levels overlap. An exceptional attacker might be a poor passer and vice versa (depending on experience, fitness, and physical attributes). Volleys will still occur after a team has progressed in practice setting up offensive plays. Simple volleying is often a part of offensive plays. The trick is to figure out what percentage of time to spend practicing volleying in addition to other types of attacks.

Following is a rough measure to determine when to move to the next skill level in practice. If a team meets the requirements to move on to the next stage seven times out of 10 (70 percent of the time), that team should start practicing skills of the next level (while still practicing the prior level skills for 30 percent of the practice and still practicing fundamental skills a portion of the time to ensure they do not regress from lack of practice). A success rate of 80 percent suggests the skills have been acquired.

Skill Building

Two alternative patterns may be used for building skills. The first possible pattern is illustrated in Figure 5-6. First, have players practice receiving and setting using drills focused on each individual skill. Then, practice drills combining the skills. Next, practice only attacking. Finally, combine all three skills with a receive-set-attack combination.

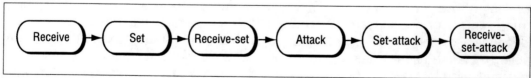

Figure 5-6. Skill progression (option 1)

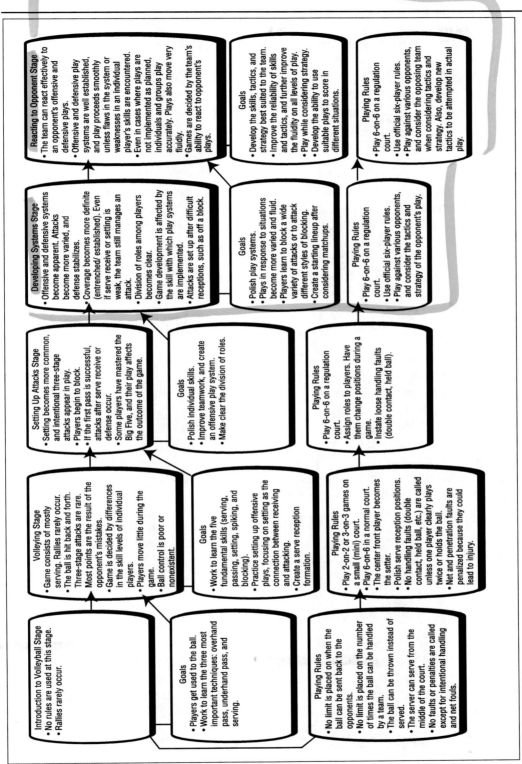

Reacting to Opponent Stage
- The team can react effectively to an opponent's offensive and defensive plays.
- Offensive and defensive play systems are well established, and play proceeds smoothly unless flaws in the system or weaknesses in an individual player's skills are encountered.
- Even in cases where plays are not implemented as planned, individuals and groups play accurately. Plays also move very fluidly.
- Games are decided by the team's ability to react to opponent's plays.

Goals
- Develop the skills, tactics, and strategy best suited to the team.
- Improve the reliability of skills and tactics, and further improve the fluidity on all levels of play.
- Play while considering strategy.
- Develop the ability to use suitable plays to score in different situations.

Playing Rules
- Play 6-on-6 on a regulation court.
- Use official six-player rules.
- Play against various opponents, and consider the opposing team when considering tactics and strategy. Also, develop new tactics to be attempted in actual play.

Developing Systems Stage
- Offensive and defensive systems become apparent. Attacks become more varied, and defense stabilizes.
- Coverage becomes more definite (entrenched/ established). Even if serve receive or setting is weak, the team still manages an attack.
- Division of roles among players becomes clear.
- Game development is affected by the skill with which play systems are implemented.
- Attacks are set up after difficult receptions, such as off a block.

Goals
- Polish play systems.
- Plays in response to situations become more varied and fluid.
- Players learn to block a wide variety of attacks or to attack different styles of blocking.
- Create a starting lineup after considering matchups.

Playing Rules
- Play 6-on-6 on a regulation court.
- Use official six-player rules.
- Play against various opponents, and consider the tactics and strategy of the opponent's play.

Setting Up Attacks Stage
- Setting becomes more common, and intentional three-stage attacks appear in play.
- Players begin to block.
- If the first pass is successful, attacks after serve receive or defense occur.
- Some players have mastered the Big Five, and their play affects the outcome of the game.

Goals
- Polish individual skills.
- Improve teamwork, and create an offensive play system.
- Make clear the division of roles.

Playing Rules
- Play 6-on-6 on a regulation court.
- Assign roles to players. Have them change positions during a game.
- Instate loose handling faults (double contact, held ball).

Volleying Stage
- Game consists of mostly serving. Rallies rarely occur.
- The ball is hit back and forth. Three-stage attacks are rare.
- Most points are the result of the opponent's mistakes.
- Game is decided by differences in the skill levels of individual players.
- Players move little during the game.
- Ball control is poor or nonexistent.

Goals
- Work to learn the five fundamental skills (serving, passing, setting, spiking, and blocking).
- Practice setting up offensive plays, focusing on setting as the connection between receiving and attacking.
- Create a serve reception formation.

Playing Rules
- Play 2-on-2 or 3-on-3 games on a small (mini) court.
- Play 6-on-6 in a normal court. The center front player becomes the setter.
- Polish serve reception positions.
- No handling faults (double contact, held ball, etc.) are called unless one player clearly plays twice or holds the ball.
- Net and penetration faults are penalized because they could lead to injury.

Introduction to Volleyball Stage
- No rules are used at this stage.
- Rallies rarely occur.

Goals
- Players get used to the ball.
- Work to learn the three most important techniques: overhand pass, underhand pass, and serving.

Playing Rules
- No limit is placed on when the ball can be sent back to the opponents.
- No limit is placed on the number of times the ball can be handled by a team.
- The ball can be thrown instead of served.
- The server can serve from the middle of the court.
- No faults or penalties are called except for intentional handling and net fouls.

Figure 5-5. Aspects of volleyball and the practice goals

This practice progression follows the natural development of volleyball skills. Another reason to use this pattern is that attacking is the most explosive and physical of volleyball skills. Early in a practice, players often have not fully warmed up. Starting a practice with attack drills easily could lead to knee, lumbar, and shoulder injuries. Rather than start practice with a dynamic attack drill, it is prudent to practice receiving and setting. After the players have warmed up, move on to attack drills. This progression is important both for a single practice session and for long-term practice plans.

The progression illustrated in Figure 5-7 is also possible, which largely reverses the progression previously described. Begin practice with individual attacking and setting drills, and then have players practice them in combination. Thereafter, practice receiving drills. Finally, practice all three skills in a receive-set-attack combination.

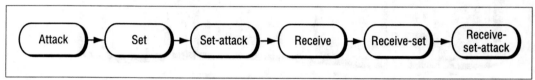

Figure 5-7. Skill progression (option 2)

This progression emphasizes attacking—the most fun skill in volleyball—and then introduces receiving as the necessary precursor for an attack. An ancient axiom in volleyball is as follows: "It all begins with a pass." Although the least dynamic or crowd-pleasing skill, passing is probably the most important fundamental skill in volleyball. Every practice must include some amount of passing. It is helpful to develop (good) game situation habits by adding an attack element to passing drills. It can motivate players in practice by having them focus first on attacking (fun) and then on receiving as the (necessary) skill to make attacking possible.

Use of this progression requires all players on a team to have mastered the five basic skills to some extent. Using this progression to teach beginners often results in an imbalance of players who can attack but who cannot receive. Such teams cannot maintain a rally and generally will lose.

Increase the Number of Drills That Include Setting

As emphasized throughout this book, skills can be built in many ways. The best drills for any skill, though, are combined with setting. Such combination drills help to improve setting skills—core to building effective offensive plays—as well as the complementary receiving and/or attacking skills necessary to start and complete an offensive play. Moreover, combination drills replicate game situations and, therefore, augment the level of play in actual games. Accordingly, have players practice as many drills as possible that combine receiving and setting, setting and attacking, and receiving, setting, and attacking.

Two Methods for Teambuilding

Once a team has started to master fundamental playing skills, the next step for improving team play is developing skills in coordination with tactics. One method involves formulating a tactical concept (the goal) and then learning the skills necessary to accomplish, achieve, or perform that concept. For example, consider a team that has conceptualized winning by using wipe-off as the primary attacking tactic. To achieve that goal, the team obviously must be able to wipe off, and, therefore, practices will focus on developing and refining that skill. This method is illustrated in the top portion of Figure 5-8. Time flows from left to right in the figure with the ultimate goal appearing at the far right endpoint of the timeline. Because the goal is introduced at the front end of the process, this method is called "the goal method" or "the thinking ahead model."

However, even if it is clear what skills are necessary to achieve a goal, they are not always learned as planned. In this case, it is necessary to use different tactics than first envisioned. For example, if the team in the previous example could not master the wipe-off but discovered during wipe-off practices a skill at tipping (the cause), the game plan would change accordingly. The team would change tactics and strategies to incorporate tipping (the effect). This approach is the second method depicted in Figure 5-8.

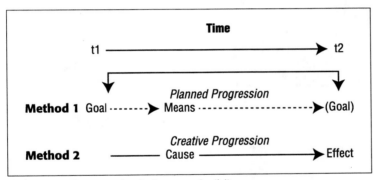

Figure 5-8. Two methods for teambuilding

The first method—in which a team sets a goal and practices the skills necessary to accomplish it—is optimal because it is clear and easily understood by the players. However, some skills cannot be perfected for various reasons, whether insufficiency of time, mental block, physical condition, or athletic ability. A coach must consider each player's strengths and weaknesses and devise tactics to utilize each player's current and anticipated skill levels.

Sometimes, a tactical or strategic plan cannot be created during the first stages of teambuilding. Indeed, this might be the most common scenario. Nonetheless, even teams unable to develop a tactical or strategic plan can be successful. As this type of team practices, the coach will spontaneously propose things for the team to try. These creative flashes can create tactics suitable for the team. Team improvement can be a deliberate process or a spontaneous one; the real secret to improving a team is to use both processes.

Drill Development

Development of drills (gradually increasing their complexity or level of difficulty) brings a team closer to its goals. The types of drills used affect both individual skills and team play, so drills must be designed to complement the team. This section will offer clues about how to match drills to team weaknesses (needs) and abilities (strengths).

A practice session consists of a number of drills designed to teach and develop skills and tactics. Logically, therefore, a coach must decide which skill or tactic to teach before selecting or designing a drill to enable the team or player(s) to master it.

In turn, coaches first collect and analyze information (technical, systematic, tactical, and strategic) about their own team and opponents to determine what skills and tactics the team needs to learn. Thereafter, coaches search for information about various drills to select or design a drill that will advance the team toward its goals. This procedure is outlined in Figure 5-9. In addition, certain basic factors must be considered in drill development (Figure 5-10).

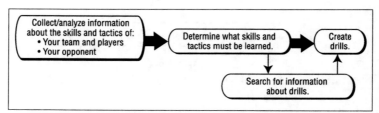

Figure 5-9. Procedure for drill development

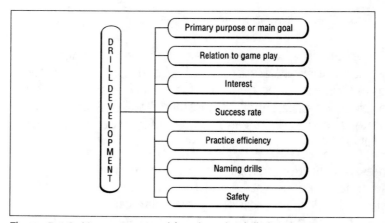

Figure 5-10. Necessary considerations in drill development

Emphasis of the Drill's Primary Purpose or Main Goal

Any drill is more effective when practiced with a clear understanding of the skills and tactics to be learned (the point of the drill). It is important to focus on the skill goals during the learning process.

Prohibit Certain Actions

- To teach players how to use knees properly in an underhand (forearm) pass, consider limiting the range of arm movement by tethering the players' arms loosely to the body.
- To teach the ready position for an underhand pass, have players practice handling the ball with the knees, not the hands.

Added Actions

- To practice positioning more quickly, require a player to make a half turn before handling the ball.
- To practice responding to a serve more quickly, have the participants start the drill lying on their stomachs in their starting positions.

Limit the Skills and Tactics

- To practice making an overhand pass/set second contact habitual, prohibit underhanded sets.
- To reinforce spiking power, prohibit tips.
- To teach quick hits and change-ups, play practice games where only these two attack patterns can be used.
- To develop back row attacks, play practice games in which all spikes must start behind the three-meter line.
- To develop the offensive ability to wipe, tip, and other alternative strategies against an imposing block, have attackers hit against two blockers standing on a table on the other side of the net.

Decrease the Number of Players

- To increase defensive range, practice with two players defending a space usually defended by three players.
- To strengthen the center front-setter combination, play 4-on-4 games with only the center front in the front line, and a setter and two other players in the back line.

Change the Court Size

- To improve attack and service control, play on a smaller court.

Change the Height of the Net

- To increase the height the ball is contacted, the height at which the ball crosses the net, or arm extension during an attack, raise the net.
- To teach the sensation of blocking properly, practice blocking with a lower net.

Relation to Game Play

A drill's effectiveness can be measured by how well it inspires players to use what they have learned. Any drill that a player feels will be useful in a game is most effective. A player who feels she can directly apply a skill in a game will work much harder to perfect it (than with drills which develop less obviously useful skills).

It is essential that the players feel that a drill is useful. Even if the coach feels that a drill is appropriate and useful, the players may not agree. It is important, therefore, that the coach communicates to the players how each drill relates to game situations.

Interest

Most players are interested in team play and eagerly practice team skills. Players tend to practice more diligently if coaches specify points on which to focus during a practice game and game situation drills.

However, it is often difficult to hold the players' interest with basic drills that repeat simple actions. To prevent loss of interest, invent ways of keeping the drills (especially for fundamental skills) interesting or competitive. By doing so, the players will be drawn into a drill and dedicate more energy to it.

For example, create drills in which players pass while playing rock-paper-scissors. Have the players head the ball to master body position for the overhand pass. Build speed in players by making them clap before they pass the ball. Make players do a somersault before they pass the ball to improve their coordination on the court. By adding small actions such as these to drills, practice becomes more interesting to players. Similarly, having groups compete to complete a drill properly and/or first, to see who can successfully complete a drill a given number of times, or to compete for points will increase players' interest and increase their desire to practice.

Success Rate

Even if players understand that a drill is useful and practice it diligently, not all skills learned will be used in a game. Only skills and tactics that are successful in practice can be applied in a game; conversely, a skill that was consistently unsuccessful in practice almost certainly will fail in competition. In other words, a drill must be designed so players at some point will successfully and consistently use a skill. In addition, practice goals should be realistic.

For example, if a beginner is told to perform 100 consecutive overhead passes, she will fail. Even if the player manages to perform 40 passes in a row, she will feel failure because the player could not complete the stated goal of 100 consecutive successful passes. In that case, the player will lack the confidence to perform an overhand pass in competition. Therefore, in drills for beginners, choose an appropriate (realistic) number of repetitions for the player to attempt (perhaps 20). By meeting such (realistic) goals, the player will be left with the sense of success and some confidence to attempt the skill in a game (and further confidence to work to improve the skill over time).

If drills are too simple, players will not feel challenged. As there will always be a stronger opponent somewhere, it is necessary to keep teams and players grounded with the knowledge and understanding that they can play better. It is necessary on occasion to run more challenging drills to inspire and motivate players to improve. An impossible drill is a confidence-breaker and fails to teach a skill. Some success rate is necessary. A success rate of 60 percent or slightly better than half is preferable. A drill with a success rate of 80 percent is too easy and one with less than 50 percent is too difficult. A success rate between 60 and 80 percent is optimal for challenging drills.

Practice Efficiency

Only so much time can be spent practicing. Practice time must be used effectively and efficiently, especially when available practice time is short.

If players practice attacking in two lines, they will repeat their attack skills twice as much than they would in one line. Similarly, if 12 players are separated into four groups of three people to practice three-player receiving drills on a full court, the players will receive twice as much passes as they would on a half court. Thus, changing the grouping or location of players can increase the frequency of repetitions completed during a given period of time.

Efficiency alone does not make a drill effective. The focus of a drill must always be its purpose. If the purpose is to practice skills and increase a player's heart rate, the drill should maximize physical activity. If the purpose, however, is to teach or develop proper skills, it becomes more important to design and run a drill in which a player can focus on each element of a skill (and, correspondingly, during which the coach can observe and correct each aspect).

Naming Drills

Naming each drill as it is learned improves practice efficiency by eliminating the need to explain the drill each time. Of course, it is necessary to explain the drill the first time, but subsequent repetition of explanations is a waste of time. By giving the drills unique names, a tremendous amount of time can be saved. Moreover, new drills based (or built) on an existing drill can be explained more quickly and easily.

Safety

Never forget safety during practice. The following points must be considered.

In the Net Area

When practicing attacking or blocking, players are often injured by jumping and landing on a ball. Set up a barrier to keep balls from rolling across the court and to create a system to pick up all loose balls.

Collisions

Lining up the players for a drill can be a problem. For example, in 1-on-1 drills, when one group lines up with a player on the base line and a player near the net, and another group lines up on either sideline (as in Figure 5-11), collisions will occur. The groups should line up facing the same direction, as depicted in Figure 5-12.

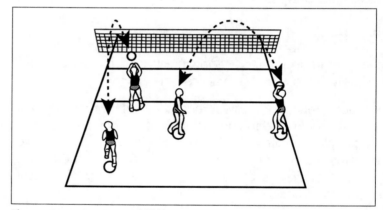

Figure 5-11. Incorrect drill lineup

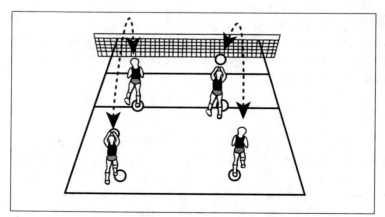

Figure 5-12. Correct drill lineup

Involving too many players in a drill simultaneously also increases the potential for collisions. When many players are on the court or involved in a drill, break into groups.

It is important to establish the area each player is responsible to protect (defend) and set up a system where only one player attempts to dig each ball. If a ball comes down between two players (as in Figure 5-13) and both players attempt to dig, they will collide. If, however, the player on the right is responsible for balls hit short and the player on the left for balls hit long, a collision is much less likely.

Figure 5-13. Establishing the court area each player is responsible to protect

Court responsibility is a tricky lesson to teach because it is far better for players to (want and be prepared to) attempt to pass a ball than to presume another player is responsible. Further, the "responsible" player will be indecisive, slow to move, or out of position at times. Consequently, teaching court responsibility also involves teaching court and situation awareness balanced with a presumption it is better to attempt to pass a ball in ambiguous situations.

Matching Plays to Player Skill Levels

If players have not mastered the basics of overhand skills, having them block attacks or overhand pass fast spiked balls could result in sprained fingers. If players lack sufficient arm strength or skill, they may strike and split their chin on the floor when diving. Players can also sprain ankles in digging drills, cutting and running after balls hit long. All of these injuries result from players attempting skills beyond their physical or technical limits. Be aware of where and how hard a ball is hit, especially during digging drills. Be conscious of the technical and physical abilities of the players when choosing drills.

Warming Up

Never begin a practice with explosive drills. Ensure players warm up and stretch. Then, ease the team into physical drills. After players are warmed up, the risk of tear, pulls, and similar injuries is greatly reduced.

Three Rules for Practices (The Three Ts)

When planning practices, coaches should pay close attention to the three Ts: theme, tempo, and teaching. Balance these factors with the skill level of the players when designing a practice.

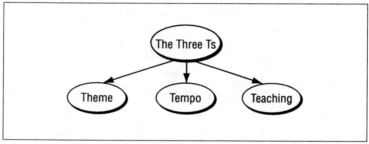

Figure 5-14. The three principles of practices

Theme

All practices need a theme (largely synonymous with a goal or goals). Elements such as polishing skills and tactics, improving physical strength, responding to psychological stress, and teamwork can be practice themes. Practices can have multiple or combined themes. Determine the goal(s) of practice, and create a practice around that theme.

Even if a practice concentrated solely on spiking, many possible themes can be implemented (Figure 5-15). Within such a practice would be themes correlating to the various skill levels of the players on the team. Practicing without a theme simply puts players through the motions.

Tempo

Tempo refers to the frequency a player contacts the ball in a given period of time. Every practice has a tempo, which changes to match factors such as the players' level, the purpose of the practice, and the composition of the team (Figure 5-16).

For example, younger or novice teams should practice the critical and difficult skills of overhead passing and serve receiving at a slow tempo, one player at a time. On the

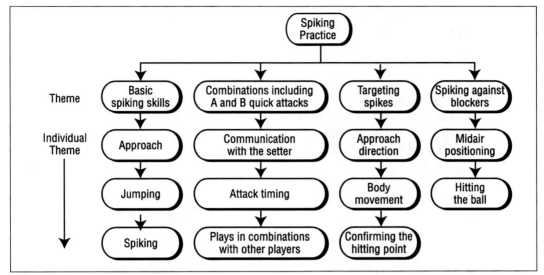

Figure 5-15. Possible spiking practice themes

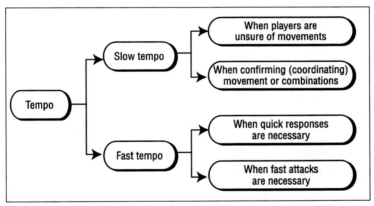

Figure 5-16. Tempo

other hand, if a practice goal is to improve player reaction or improve early spiking skills, high-tempo practices are better.

A change in the tempo of a frequent drill can change the feel of a practice. Try changing the tempo to match various purposes (e.g., skill refinement versus reaction).

Teaching

When planning a practice, it is vital to consider how the practice ties in to the development of skill. Generally, coaches should teach how a skill is applied (used in competition) only after players have mastered the basic elements of the skill.

Figure 5-17 illustrates the patterns for basic digging practice. First, players learn to be in the ready position while waiting for the ball to enter the court. Then, have players practice the various digging forms (overhand, forearm underhand, dive, pancake) for passing or handling an incoming ball. Initially, balls should be hit/served to or near players so they develop confidence, consistency, and proper form. As players become proficient, increase the speed of the hit/serve or the distance from the players to challenge the players and further refine their digging and passing skills. Finally, it is necessary to teach players to think about the next play while handling the ball. Many practice patterns can be employed, including practicing the rhythm of movements or taking the eyes off the ball to watch the opposing team.

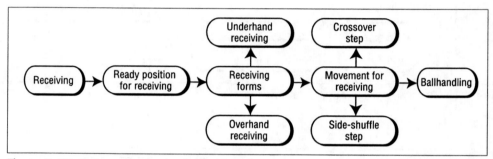

Figure 5-17. Patterns for basic digging practice

Drill Types

Drill Tempo

Teaching Tempo

To teach new skills, conduct practice at a slow tempo, one play at a time. Use the time between each play to give feedback about the reasons a skill was (or was not) successful.

Fast Tempo

To maximize ball contact or increase movement speed (reaction), conduct drills at a fast tempo. Practicing at this speed prepares players for the high tempo of competition. Indeed, conducting some drills or practices at a tempo even faster than game situations can give players confidence they can compete at the (slower) game tempo. Be careful about using too fast a practice tempo with beginning players, who can become intimidated or lose focus.

Game Tempo

Actual games feature a variety of tempos, from the slow pace of a teaching tempo (e.g., a free ball) to the blur of high-level competition (a spike inside the three-meter line). It is helpful, therefore, to polish skills at a variety of speeds. The most effective method to practice multiple tempos is to use practice games and drills replicating game situations.

The Number of Skills to Be Learned in a Drill—Single-Skill Drills and Compound Drills

In practice, single-skill drills attempt to impart a single skill. Compound drills attempt to develop multiple skills (such as receiving and attacking) in the same drill.

Single-Skill Drills

These drills attempt to teach and develop one single skill's form and application through repetition. A common single-skill drill to teach digging begins with the digger receiving strong, deep hits followed by hits to the left or right. Finally, practice digging tips.

Compound Drills

Compound drills endeavor to improve an individual's ability to perform multiple skills in succession. A common example of this type of drill incorporates receiving (passing) a serve, attacking, and then jumping to block the opponent's return. In addition to practicing the discrete skills, this drill develops the ability to transition smoothly between skills. Competition is filled with transitions. Consequently, compound drills are vital to teach players how to apply, and transition between, skills in game situations.

Drilling Play Patterns—Patterned Drills and Improvisation Drills

Patterned Drills

Teams often develop special plays or systems for specific game situations (e.g., free balls, shanked passes, setter passing). Pattern drills practice such plays as player and ball movement is decided before the drill is conducted.

Improvisation Drills

Conversely, competition is fluid and one team can influence but never fully control the performance and actions of its opponent. Therefore, teams must be able to adapt and improvise for those many times in a game when a predetermined play will not work. Improvisational drills do not have a predetermined pattern but, rather, require players to make the plays they think most appropriate in response to conditions. This type of drill develops flexibility and adaptability in competition.

Linking Skills in Drills—Individual Practice, Group Practice, and Team Practice

As explained previously in this chapter, individual skills, group skills, and team skills generally are learned in that order. Therefore, practices can be classified as individual practice, group practice, and team practice.

Individual Practice

Sometimes, it is necessary to focus on individual players in a practice (e.g., to develop a new setter or move an outside hitter to the middle blocker position), usually in the form of single-player drills. Because a player receives individualized instruction, that player's individual skills should improve more quickly than in a group practice. This type of practice tends to be inefficient because there are usually many more players than coaches and undirected players waste time standing around or practicing less productive drills. In planning a practice when there will be individualized instruction, pay extra attention to how the remaining members of the team will be kept active, engaged, and productive.

Group Practice

Group practices consist of drills involving multiple (two or more) players practicing ballhandling (how to handle the ball when passing or setting in receive-set and set-attack combinations) and developing combination plays. A large percentage of every practice should be dedicated to group drills.

Team Practice

Team drills involve a full team (six-player) on one or both sides of the net. Their purpose is to practice and develop passing, setting, and attacking skills under game conditions.

Practice Organization—Coach-Oriented and Player-Oriented Drills

Practice organization refers to who is implementing and leading the drills. Coaches or players can lead drills.

Practice Conducted by the Coach

When coaches hit the ball into play for the players to receive, set, or attack, the coaches set and modify the tempo or conditions of the drill as they deem appropriate to teach, develop, and challenge the players.

Practice Conducted By the Players

For a drill conducted only by the players to succeed, the players must possess a certain level of skill and the player(s) leading the drill must possess (and be recognized by their teammates as possessing) leadership qualities.

The Net—Practicing With and Without a Net

Even though volleyball is a net sport, it is possible to learn basic skills without a net. However, once players have attained the most basic skill level, they must pay attention to the other side of the court to improve. Accordingly, most or all practices will necessitate the use of nets.

Using a net identifies and even emphasizes the opponent's side of the court, while the absence of a net would downplay the presence of an opponent. If simple forms have been established, some skills that usually require a net such as attacking, blocking, and digging can occasionally be practiced without a net. However, blocking or receiving an opponent's attack and attacking against an opponent's block are best practiced with a net and multiple players (up to a full team) on each side.

Court Size—Practicing on a Full Court, Half Court, or in a Smaller Space

An indoor volleyball court is 9 by 18 meters. However, practicing on a smaller court (badminton court or half-court size) to play a 2-on-2 or 3-on-3 game can compel better ball control (and related skill development) or facilitate transition to six-player games on a full-sized court. Smaller practice courts can also help advanced players develop finer or more difficult skills.

Rallies—Practicing With and Without Rallies

Drills that allow rallies mirror the variability of actual game situations, while non-rally drills tend to involve far less variability. For beginning players, stop-and-go drills at a teaching tempo facilitate learning the five basic skills. In drills that involve rallies, basic skills are often neglected. Conversely, drills that prohibit rallies promote the development and refinement of discrete skills.

On the other hand, drills which include rallies impart the movements, ball control, and play coordination of game situations. Because these drills can be adapted to any number of players (up to a full team of six), they are easily modified to address diverse goals, whether development of individual player skills, development of teamwork and transition, or a combination of goals.

Drills Suitable for Different Themes

Through experience, education, and trial/error, coaches learn to choose or design a drill effective for the practice theme they have selected. Figure 5-18 summarizes the types of drills and the themes listed in this section. It should help when creating or selecting drills.

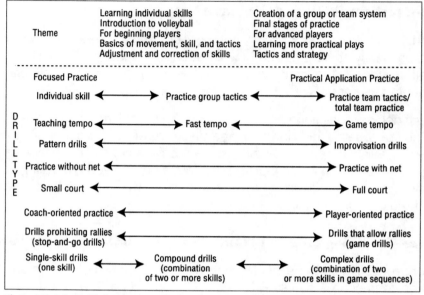

Figure 5-18. Drill themes and types

Methods for Establishing Objectives

As stated, it is critical to develop drills that will help individuals or teams to achieve their goals. For this reason, it is important to identify (and communicate) drill objectives.

Setting Objectives for Drills

Stated simply, setting objectives is the same as determining when a drill will end. Practices should end a drill on a positive note (i.e., when players believe a drill was completed successfully). Thus, setting realistic (achievable) objectives is an important factor in developing drills. Methods for establishing objectives include:

- *Number of repetitions:* Identify a number of repetitions to be completed.
  - ✓ Example: Hit 20 consecutive spikes.
- *Number of successes:* Establish the number of times a drill must be successfully completed.
  - ✓ Example: Make five successful blocks.

- *Number of consecutive successes:* Establish a number of consecutive repetitions to be completed successfully.
  - ✓ Example: In three-player digging drills, prevent a ball hit by the coach from contacting the floor 20 consecutive times.
- *Time limit:* Establish a clear duration for a (difficult or strenuous) drill. Time limits are especially meaningful for explosive or high-energy drills as they mentally enable a player to exert maximum effort for the stated period.
  - ✓ Example: Continue attacking for three minutes.
- *Number of successes with a time limit:* Establish a number of repetitions to be completed successfully within a given period.
  - ✓ Example: Complete 30 successful passes in five minutes.
- *Performance percentage:* Have players try to achieve a predetermined performance percentage (i.e., successful repetitions / total repetitions x 100). By using this formula, performance of skills such as spiking, serving, or setting can be quantified.
  - ✓ Example: In serve receiving practice, set an objective of seven good passes out of 10 (70 percent). A poor score often serves as its own penalty.
- *Plus/minus points:* Set a score for players to achieve, and have players practice until they reach that score. Award points for successful plays, and deduct points for unsuccessful ones (for plays which should have been completed successfully).
  - ✓ Example: In spiking practice, award one point for successful spikes, no points for spikes that are dug, and deduct one point for missed spikes (balls hit in the net or out-of-bounds). Continue until a player has scored 10 points.

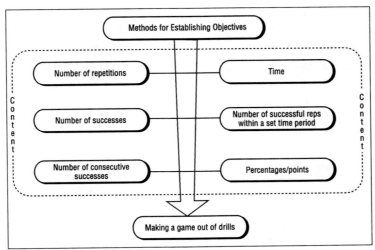

Figure 5-19. Methods for establishing objectives

Multiple Players

Multi-player drills help players develop a sense of teamwork and cooperative attitude. Coaches should encourage an individual player's motivation to succeed to support their teammates (and sometimes to avoid squandering a teammate's previous good or "heroic" play).

Quantity and Quality

Drills with a set number of repetitions or a time limit are effective when coaches believe a large number of repetitions are necessary. When emphasizing play quality, it is better to specify the number of successful completions required to end the drill. In either case, repetition solidifies and polishes plays.

Penalties

To stop bad habits and encourage good ones, coaches sometimes impose a penalty for failed drills (or clearly below average effort). Penalties can be a good method for motivating players and intensifying player concentration. Penalties that are too severe can undermine the trust or general relationship between players and the coach. If a player is inexperienced or already self-critical to an extreme, penalties can lower motivation instead of heightening it. Effective coaches wear many hats, including and especially psychologist, as they must learn what motivate or inspires each player on a roster.

- In competitive drills, replace the losing team (especially in fun drills) which returns to the practice line to await (eagerly) the chance to return to the court.
- With psychologically strong teams, have a drill continue until every player has completed a skill successfully an identified number of times (e.g., 20 passes to the target zone).
- During pre-season or early in a season, have players who do not achieve practice goals run laps or perform certain exercises (developing greater fitness and endurance).

Pressure

In plus/minus point drills, players are motivated to avoid mistakes, which helps players learn to compete under stress. In actual games, players feel pressure when facing a strong opponent or arch rival, playing a particularly tall or well-jumping team, when behind in the score, or when teammates are not playing well. To accustom players to function under such psychological conditions, it is important to conduct some drills that induce stress.

Making a Game Out of Drills

Drills can have many possible objectives. Converting a drill into a game can increase the benefits (objectives accomplished) for that drill. For example, identify a zone that players should target when serving and challenge the team to see which player can be the first to land 10 serves in the zone. Alternatively, create two teams of three players, and have them compete to see which team makes the most successful (accurate) passes in three minutes. Such drills teach skills to players while enjoying, and being motivated by, the friendly competition.

Setting Objectives for Practice Games

Practice objectives are usually controlled by the rules of the game. Indeed, it is instructive to practice under standard game rules. On occasion, though, it can be helpful to play/practice under special rules to emphasize a particular lesson.

Conclusion of a Game

Practice games can end at a set score or after a set period of time.

• Playing to a predetermined score

Under standard rules, a team wins a game or set when it has scored 25 points and is ahead by at least two points (otherwise, the first team to pull ahead by two points wins). It is not necessary to adhere to the 25-point game, and the final score of a practice game or drill can be five, seven, or 10 points, as appropriate.

In some situations, the game's score can change a team's mindset and tactics. As players become more advanced, these psychological and tactical changes can affect the outcome of a game. Therefore, it is necessary for players to learn how to select appropriate plays and to modify their psychological state. Normally, practice games start with a score of 0-0, but there are other options. For example, players can have a five-point game to practice scoring points early in the game. A game can start with a score of 20-20 to practice scoring the final five points (psychologically "closing out" the match). Consider starting with a score of 12-14 (as in the match point of a fifth game or set), to learn how to come back from behind (and successfully compete under pressure).

• Timed games

When a time limit is set, teams compete to score the most points within a given time period. This method is most effective when the time allotted or available for practice is limited and, therefore, is often used in school physical education classes. Timed practice games lose some effectiveness when the outcome is obvious and moderate to substantial time is left in the game (e.g., with five minutes left to play, there is a 10-point difference) and the (desired) feeling or motivation of pressure disappears.

Advanced players thrive on competition. They lose motivation and have less fun when the outcome becomes obvious. However, competition is less important for developmental players who simply enjoy playing, regardless of the score. Consequently, timed games are more appropriate for beginning players. Timed drills can be useful for advanced players, if score is not kept. Without a score, players focus on polishing skills and tactics, making timed drills suitable for refining play systems or introducing new ones.

Methods of Keeping Score

In a six-player, five-set match, the standard format is for points to be scored by a rally-point system; sometimes, changing scoring methods improves a practice's efficiency or helps to meet objectives.

- Side-out system: Only the serving team can score points in this (old, but original) method of volleyball scoring.
- Rally-point system: A point is awarded to the team winning each rally, regardless of who served.

The following alternative methods of scoring can have practice benefits:
- Bonus-point system: Points awarded are doubled or tripled when the skills being practiced are used effectively. For example, award two points for effective three-stage attacks, three points for effective blocking, or adjust bonus points for coed teams.
- Sudden death system: If a team successfully utilizes the skill or tactic that was the practice's objective, the set is awarded to the team that used it. For example, when conducting a practice game to learn a specific attack pattern, the first team to score a point using that attack wins, and the game is over. Score can be kept or not, as the coach deems best. However, the team that successfully uses the skill or tactic instantly wins, regardless of the score before the play was made.
- Wash point system: In this system, a team scores small (contingent) points upon successfully completing a play. Should the team score two consecutive points, it is awarded a big (real) point (one point). If the other team scores the following point, the small point (of the first team) is a wash (erased), and the teams start the next play even. Thus, the team which was behind by a contingent point is now only even. When playing under the wash system, even a five-point game becomes quite intense.
- Handicapping system: When the teams' skill levels are different, award extra points to the weaker team (double points or starting with a lead).
- King's court (or queen's court) (Figure 5-20): This is not actually a method of scoring, but it is listed here as a method to increase player interest in practice games. Create several teams and have two teams play a game to a predetermined score. The winning team stays in (or moves to) court A, and the next team moves

to (or stays in) court B. Because the winning team always plays in court A, that court is known as the king's court or queen's court. Should one team remain in the king's or queen's court for a set number of games, that team is declared the king or queen of the practice. This drill might seem like a child's game, but it allows players to compete, earn bragging rights, and have fun. This drill is best played with two- or three-player teams because several teams are necessary.

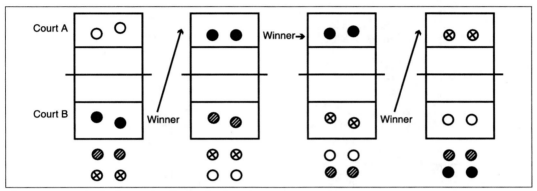

Figure 5-20. King's Court (or Queen's Court)

Figure 5-21 summarizes these scoring methods and the characteristics for each. These methods are not set in stone or exclusive. The point is that a coach should think about the characteristics of each scoring method and use the method most appropriate for the goals of a practice or drill.

Developing Acumen in Coaches and Players

Coaches must learn or be able to judge player skill levels. This ability enables a coach to evaluate the quality of a team's performance and determine whether to continue practicing a drill or move on (progress) to another.

In addition, a coach must learn or be able to determine a team's physical and psychological condition by watching players' faces, movements, and behavior. Exceptional coaches have an eye for both skill and a team's condition.

Players, too, must learn to judge their own performance objectively. To do so, players must make full use of their senses, from their sense of limb placement, sense of speed, sense of distance (to the ball and to other players) and sense of their strength. Of course, statistical consistency in competition is generally an objective measure.

An unspoken axiom posits: "A drill should end when the skill it teaches has been mastered." It is helpful for players and coaches to be able to judge skills, performance, and when to stop practicing a drill. The decision ultimately belongs to the coach, who is responsible for preparing a team to compete at its maximum potential.

Characteristics					
	Time	*Player intensity level*	*Appropriate for teams with different skill levels*	*Suitable for learning skills and tactics*	*Suitable for learning plays that appear in a game*
Game Format					
Timed game	As preferred	Medium	No	Depending on the objective	No
Scored games:					
Side-out system	Long	High when competing for points	No	Depending on the objective	Yes
Rally-point system	Short	High (someone will score on every play)	Yes	Depending on the objective	Yes
Bonus-point system	Short	Medium/high (players are competing to win bonus points)	Yes	Yes	Somewhat
Wash-point system	Long	High	Yes	Depending on the objective	Somewhat
Handicap system	Long	High	Yes with handicaps in place	Depending on the objective	Somewhat
Sudden death system	Unpredictable	High (unclear when the game will end)	Yes because victory could come at anytime	Well-suited if the skill is made clear	No

Figure 5-21. Methods of scoring and their characteristics

6

Conditioning for Volleyball: Understanding the Basics

To a certain extent, great athletes are born, not made. In that regard, the best thing a want-to-be superstar could do would be to choose her parents wisely. Despite the extravagant claims made for this particular workout program or that particular wonder drug, all athletes are "blessed" or "cursed" with characteristics that no barbell, exercise regimen, or dietary supplement can change.

In point of fact, a higher level of overall fitness, particularly muscular fitness, will provide volleyball players with at least two fundamental benefits: reduced injury potential and enhanced performance potential. While these effects can help individuals of all ages and interests, they are very important to those whop lay sports. Given the dynamic, somewhat volatile nature of volleyball, players are sometimes exposed to a high risk of injury during a contest. Uncontrolled motion, external forces, sudden stops, immovable objects, and above-average velocity are a few factors that can result in an athlete being injured. On the other hand, players who increase the fitness level of a muscle and its connective tissues (tendons and ligaments) will be less endangered by these risks. As such, every volleyball player should view conditioning, especially strength training, as a sound and inexpensive form of health insurance.

Volleyball players should also keep in mind how conditioning can enhance their performance. For example, a higher level of muscular fitness will not increase their fatigue threshold, but also enable the muscle to recover more quickly and efficiently. As the great former basketball coach of UCLA, John Wooden, once said: "In any close contest, in any sport, conditioning will be the key to victory." Having their muscles ready and able to do what they want at any moment can be a critical factor for athletes achieving success. Conditioning can play a crucial role in determining whether an athlete's muscles "can do" or have to "make do."

Function at the Junction

In addition to genetic factors and a well-designed and implemented conditioning program, the ability to perform selected motor functions influences how well individuals do athletically. Collectively, these functions are defined as motor ability. Individually, each plays a role in athletic performance (definitions of the basic motor functions follow). For many athletes, a high level of ability in these motor functions can make the difference between success and failure. To a limited extent, volleyball players can affect their ability to perform the various motor functions through conditioning (particularly strength training, because each function involves movement) and practice (resulting in a higher level of neuromuscular efficiency).

Definitions of the Basic Motor Functions

- *Agility* is the ability to change directions rapidly and effectively, while moving at a high rate of speed.
- *Balance* is the ability to maintain a specific body position, while either stationary or moving.
- *Coordination* is the smooth, desired flow of movement in the execution of a motor task. Forceful and explosive movements are blended with accurate and less forceful movements to achieve purposeful movement.
- *Kinesthetic sense* is the ability to be aware of the positions of various parts of the body. It is particularly important in athletics.
- *Movement time* is the time required to move part of the body from one point to another.
- *Reaction time* is the time required to initiate a response to a stimulus.
- *Response time* is movement time plus reaction time.
- *Speed* is the time required to move the entire body from one place to another.

Athletic Program Considerations

Although the need for conditioning may be more obvious for athletes than nonathletes, the approach and techniques for the two groups are essentially the same. How individuals, for example, develop a muscle doesn't change because they're an athlete. The fundamentals, techniques, and principles involved in sound conditioning are as important to the nonathlete as to the sportswoman.

Two issues that volleyball players must consider, which may or may not apply to nonathletes, are the need for seasonal program adjustments and the need to develop the muscles that are involved in their sport. Most strength training programs for athletes include seasonal adjustments in their design. For example, many athletes strength train twice a week during the season and three times a week during the off-season. Other athletes cut back on the number of exercises performed during an in-season workout. In the interest of conserving time, some split their workouts during the season (upper-body exercises one day and lower-body exercises the next, instead of whole-body workouts on nonconsecutive days). As a rule, the relative intensity of the workouts remains the same. Only the net amount of exercise is diminished. Whatever their preference, it is recommended that volleyball players not strength train for 36 hours before competing.

It is essential that volleyball players ensure that their resistance training program includes exercises to develop the musculature involved in their sport. As such, the first step is to identify what muscles are involved in volleyball. Table 6-1 provides a list of muscle groups employed in volleyball. Figures 6-1 and 6-2 show the anterior and posterior muscles of the body.

Fundamental Techniques	
Basic Skills	**Muscles Involved**
1. Jumping	Buttocks, quadriceps, hamstrings
2. Serving	Deltoids, trapezius, latissimus dorsi
3. Setting	Pectorals, deltoids, triceps, biceps
4. Spiking	Deltoids, triceps, forearm flexors, latissimus dorsi
5. Digging	Biceps, latissimus dorsi, trapezius, pectorals
6. Blocking	Deltoids, latissimus dorsi, trapezius
7. Sprinting	Buttocks, quadriceps, hamstrings, adductors, abductors
Potential Problem Areas:	
• Muscular endurance	
• Stamina	
• Shoulder injuries	
• Leg muscle strains	
Areas to Emphasize:	
• Use a comprehensive running/interval program to develop stamina.	
• Develop muscles that are critical to the performance of basic volleyball skills.	
• Emphasize flexibility conditioning.	
• Develop musculature of the shoulder girdle and legs.	
• Develop knee joint stability.	

Table 6-1. Conditioning for volleyball

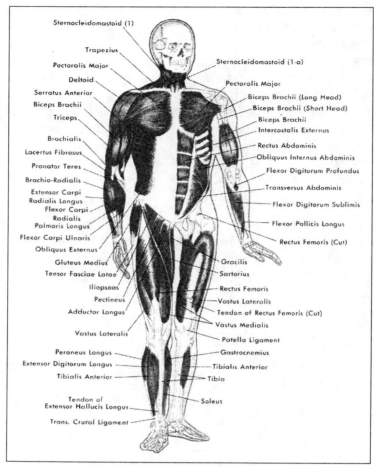

Figure 6-1. Muscles of the body (anterior view)

Components of Fitness

Depending upon whether or not muscular fitness is viewed as being one or two of the primary aspects of fitness, four (perhaps five) qualities are basic to physical fitness. As such, in order to achieve the essential benefits that are attendant to conditioning, volleyball players need to address each of the following components of fitness:

- *Cardiovascular fitness* is that aspect of fitness which enables an individual to engage in strenuous activity for extended periods of time. Dependent upon the combined efficiency of the heart, circulatory vessels, and lungs, cardiovascular fitness is an integral factor in an athlete's performance in sports that involve the use of much of the body's large musculature (volleyball, for example). The reason for this situation is that sports in which the large muscles of the body are extensively utilized require that the heart, lungs, and circulatory vessels operate at greater than

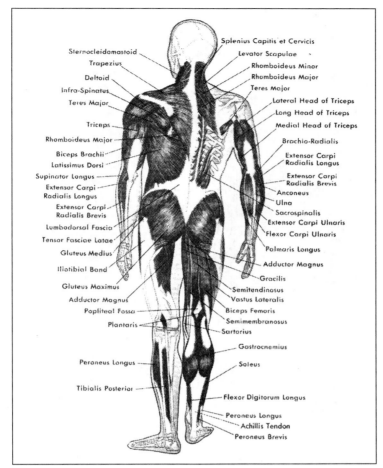

Figure 6-2. Muscles of the body (posterior view)

usual levels of efficiency. When the circulatory and respiratory systems of athletes fail to meet the cardiovascular demands of their sport, their performance suffers.

- *Muscular fitness* is that attribute which enables an individual to engage in activities requiring greater-than-normal levels of muscular development. The literature is equivocal, however, concerning the "nature" of muscular development. Some individuals claim that such development is inclusive in that it encompasses both of the two basic applications of muscular work—endurance and force. Other individuals argue that although the ability to persist in a localized muscle group activity (endurance) and the ability to exert force (strength) are interrelated, the two factors are separate, distinct qualities of fitness. "Muscular endurance" can be defined as that aspect of muscular fitness which enables an individual to engage in localized muscle group activities (e.g., serving the volleyball, moving to set the volleyball, etc.) for an extended period of time with relative, comparable effectiveness. "Muscular strength" is the maximum amount of force that can be exerted by a muscle or

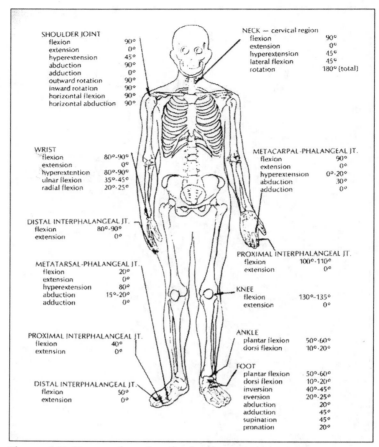

Figure 6-3. Range of motion for fundamental movements
(anterior view)

muscle group. It is specific to a given muscle or muscle group and is related to the nature of the resistance (i.e., whether it is movable—dynamic or isotonic or fixed—isometric, for example, spiking the volleyball (movable).

- *Flexibility* is the functional capacity of a joint to move through a normal range of motion. It is specific to given joints and is dependent primarily on the musculature surrounding a joint. Figures 6-3 and 6-4 illustrate the "normal" range of motion for the majority of the joints in the body. Both common sense and recent research lend credence to the importance of flexibility in all forms of sport, including volleyball.

- *Body composition* is an indicator of the amount of fat stored in the body. It is an important quality of fitness for the athlete because considerable evidence exists that excess fat stored in the body can limit an athlete's performance. Normal values of fat as a percentage of total body weight vary between men and women. The *upper* limit of "normal" for men is 18 percent and for women 28 percent. All factors considered, no established minimal levels for body fat have been determined. If an

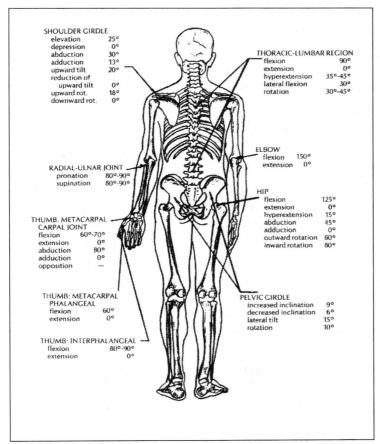

Figure 6-4. Range of motion for fundamental movements (posterior view)

athlete receives adequate nutrition, it is not possible for that person to be *too* lean. Different sports require varying proportions of body fat for maximum performance. For volleyball, for example, a minimum amount of fat is desirable.

Participants in other activities, such as distance running, high jumping, and gymnastics, also benefit from having a relatively minimal level of body fat, since athletes in those sports are generally hindered by the added weight. On the other hand, a few athletes (distance swimmers, for example) can be aided by having a basic amount of fat distributed near the skin surface to diminish the heat loss to water.

The Three Most Important Principles of Conditioning

Volleyball players who want to get the most of their conditioning efforts must adhere to certain principles. If they do not, they may well benefit from their conditioning activities, just not to the degree that they could or should. Regardless of the sport, the following three principles are absolutely essential to achieving maximal results from conditioning:

- *Demand* expresses the principle that in order for substantial improvement to occur in a system of the body or in a quality of physical fitness, the system must be stressed beyond its normal limits. If a demand is not placed on a system, no improvement will occur in that system. For example, athletes who can curl 30 lbs will not improve the strength of their biceps muscle by curling 20 lbs. By the same token, a five-minute miler will not break the five-minute barrier by practicing six-minute miles. It is important to note that physiological responses occur within the body because of a particular need for that particular response.

- *Specificity* expresses the principle that "you get what you work for." In other words, for volleyball players who wish to improve a specific skill or capability, the best method is to practice that activity. In other words, nothing replaces the activity itself for the athlete who wants to improve her ability to perform the activity.

- The *S.E.E. principle* expresses the point that the three key focal areas of any conditioning program must be safety, effectiveness, and efficiency. Nothing must compromise the overall safety of the activity. In turn, every effort must be made to maximize the results of the efforts. Finally, the amount of time devoted to perform the program should be minimized.

Types of Training

Depending upon an individual's existing level of fitness, as well as the time and equipment available, a volleyball player should develop a conditioning program that incorporates several of the following types of training:

- *Acceleration sprinting* involves running, with a gradual increase in speed from jogging to sprinting. For example, an individual might jog 25 meters, run at one-quarter to one-half speed for 25 meters, and then sprint for 50 meters.

- *Continuous fast running* involves running at a pace that is faster than in slow running; it is designed to allow the body to adapt to increasing workloads.

- *Fartlek training* involves informal slow-fast running over varied terrain; combines all forms of training.

- *Interval running** involves running with only incomplete recovery (jogging) between workouts. Workouts are submaximal in intensity. Two basic types of intervals exist:

  ✓ *Fast interval* is well suited for a pre-season regimen, where specificity and anaerobic power are paramount. The intensity of the work in a fast interval is greater than a slow interval (three-quarters speed). The athlete should jog during the relief interval. The heart rate should reach approximately 80 BPM after successive intervals.

  ✓ *Slow interval* refers to formal fast-slow running. The work interval is accomplished at roughly one-half to three-quarters speed, and the heart rate should reach approximately 180 BPM after successive workouts. Jogging is done during the relief interval and normally is three time the duration of the work interval. The intensity of the work interval is greater than in continuous fast running.

- *Interval sprinting* involves short sprints (50 to 60 meters), followed by jogging (20 to 30 meters, followed again by sprints for two to three miles total distance).
- *Jog-sprint training* involves sprinting, followed by jogging an equal distance between the sprints.
- *Long slow-distance running* involves running long distances at a slow pace (jogging); the heart rate should be around 140 to150 BPM.
- *Plyometric training** involves linking strength with speed of movement to produce power (also referred to as "jump training").
- *Repetition running* involves running distances generally from one-half to three miles with complete recovery (walking) in between.
- *Repetition sprinting* involves maximum performance over short distances, with near complete recovery (pulse dropping below 120 BPM).
- *Strength training** involves placing an appropriate demand on the muscles in order to increase the muscle's level of fitness (i.e., ability to adapt to and handle that demand).
- *Stretching** involves the process of elongating connective tissues and muscles, as well as other tissues.

In reality, volleyball players can design and engage in a conditioning program that best suits their needs and interests. At a minimum, their conditioning efforts should include the four types of training noted with an asterisk (*): interval training, plyometric training, strength training, and stretching.

Putting It All Together

In reality, developing a conditioning program for volleyball can be a relatively complicated undertaking, given the myriad of opinions that exist on the topic and the complexity of the array of training regimens that tend to be advocated by those who think that they're in the know, versus those who really do know what they're talking about. Truth be known, in order to be effective, a conditioning program does not have to either complex or costly. In fact, in most situations, it is far better for it to simply be straightforward and relatively low or no cost.

With regard to how to best organize and implement a conditioning program for volleyball, certain factors should be considered and adopted (if at all possible):

- Athletes must train during the season as well as during the off-season.
- The volume of in-season training should be noticeably less than the off-season regimen (e.g., two workouts per week versus three per week).
- If aerobic work (i.e., running) is to be performed on the same day as strength training, athletes should do the resistance training last.

- Warm-up, warm-down, and stretching activities should be performed every day at practice (as well as before and after games, if time permits).
- As a rule, all strength and stretching exercises should be performed under control (as opposed to ballistically).
- All factors considered, athletes don't need expensive equipment to strength train. More often than not, body-weight training is just as effective, if not more so.
- While what athletes eat will not make them champion-like caliber performers, it can easily prevent them from performing at their best.
- Strength training is not a contest. The rule of thumb is to "do your best and leave the rest."
- The degree to which athletes develop larger muscles is largely beyond the control of the individuals themselves. As a rule, it is virtually impossible for women athletes to develop large muscles.
- The primary goal of strength training should be to develop strength, not demonstrate it.
- Athletes who generally eat a nutritionally sound diet and take supplements are wasting their time and their money. The only exception would be if a physician prescribed the dietary supplements.

Sample Programs

The number of possible conditioning programs for volleyball that could be developed is virtually endless. Tables 6-2 to 6-4 illustrate a sample program for plyometric training, strength training, and stretching.

Warm-up Activities:	Exercises:
1. Marching-in-place drills	1. Multiple box-to-box squat jumps
2. Jogging-in-place drills	2. Depth jumps
3. Skipping drills	3. Split-squat jumps
4. Footwork/agility drills	4. Rim jumps
5. Lunging drills	5. 90-second box drill

Guidelines:

- Beginners should do 60 to 100 foot contacts (i.e., the number of times a foot hits the ground) of low-intensity exercises and 100 foot contacts of moderate-intensity exercises during the same cycle. Intermediate exercisers should perform 100 to 150 foot contacts of low-intensity exercises and 100 foot contacts of moderate-intensity exercises during the same cycle, which advanced exercisers might do 150 to 250 foot contacts of low-to-moderate-intensity exercises during the same cycle.
- Exercisers should schedule two to three days between plyometric training sessions.
- Plyometric training should be part of an overall conditioning program that also includes strength training and sprint or interval training.
- As a rule, one to two sets of 10 to 20 repetitions of each exercise are suggested for each workout. Whether such a training regimen is appropriate for a particular athlete is subject to a number of variables.

For additional information on plyometric training, refer to the book *Jumping Into Plyometrics* by Don Chu (Champaign, IL: Human Kinetics, 1998).

Table 6-2. Sample plyometric training program

Exercise	Primary Muscles Developed	Specific Skills Involved
1. Leg Press	Buttocks, quadriceps	Running, jumping
2. Leg Extension	Quadriceps	Running, jumping
3. Leg Curl	Hamstrings	Running
4. Bench Press	Pectorals, deltoids, triceps	Setting, spiking
5. Chin-ups	Latissimus dorsi, biceps	Spiking, digging, blocking
6. Seated press	Deltoids, triceps	Spiking, setting, blocking
7. Lat Pulldowns	Latissimus dorsi, biceps	Spiking
8. Triceps Extension	Triceps	Spiking
9. Wrist Curls	Forearm flexors	Spiking, setting, wrist control
10. Shrugs	Trapezius	Serving, spiking, setting, blocking

- Perform at least one set of 8 to 12 reps of each exercise during each workout.
- Take no more than 60 seconds to perform each set.
- Rest no more than 30 seconds between each set.
- To determine total workout time, multiply number of workouts by 1 1/2 minutes. Then subtract 30 seconds from the total.

Table 6-3. Sample strength training program for volleyball

Exercises:
1. One leg bent forward, one leg straight behind the other leg, push against the wall.
2. Standing on step, toes only on the step, and raise the heels.
3. Seated, one leg tucked in, one leg extended straight out, forward stretch.
4. Seated, legs straight and wide apart, bend forward to one side, and grab the foot.
5. Stand next to the wall, brace against the wall with one hand, and pull the heel of one foot with a hand toward the buttocks.
6. Lying down flat, grasp a knee with the same-side hand and the ankle of that leg with the opposite hand, and pull the foot toward the opposite shoulder.
7. Sit on a chair with legs slightly apart, bend upper torso forward as far as possible.
8. Sit on the floor with knees slightly flexed, lean forward and pull back on the thigh, keeping the feet on the floor.
9. Stand with one arm flexed behind the back, grasp the elbow of that arm with the opposite hand and pull it.
10. Stand in an open doorway, raise the arms to shoulder height, place the palms against the walls, and stretch the ribcage.
11. Sit on a chair sideways next to a table, rest the forearm on the table, with the elbow flexed, and bend forward lowering the head and shoulder to the table.
12. Stand with one arm behind the back, positioned as far up as possible, flex the other arm overhead, with the elbow flexed, interlock the fingers with each hand, and pull.
Guidelines:
• Perform each stretch statically, as opposed to ballistically.
• Stretch all of the major areas of the body daily at practice or before games.
• Perform two to three repetitions of each exercise.
• Hold each stretch for 10 to 30 seconds.
• Stretch to the point of discomfort, not pain.
Additional information on proper stretching can be found in the book *Sport Stretch, 2nd Edition* by Jonathan Alter (Champaign, IL: Human Kinetics, 1998).

Table 6-4. Sample stretching program

7

Rules Guide

The rules of volleyball vary with the number of players on the court (doubles, triples, quads, sixes), age group, court surface (beach versus indoors), and player gender. The FIVB revises the rules with each Olympics. The rules for volleyball have changed drastically from those used at the Tokyo Olympics in 1964, when volleyball was introduced as an Olympic event. This chapter will explain some of the basic indoor rules of volleyball in effect as of the date of this publication. Certain countries further revise the rules for domestic competition. Within certain countries, academic organizations vary the rules even further. Under any circumstance, rules are generally changed to lengthen rallies (keep the ball moving) and increase player and spectator interest in the game.

Team: Six players compete on one team.

Scoring and winning: A point is awarded when either team wins a rally or when the opposing team commits a foul. A game is called a set. A set continues until a team scores 25 points and has a two-point lead. Matches are played in a best-of-five format; the first team to win three sets captures the match. When both teams have won two sets, the first team to reach 15 points (a shorter set) with at least a two-point lead wins the fifth set and the match. To ensure fair play in the fifth set, the teams switch courts after one team has attained eight points.

Faults

Penalty: The serve and a point is awarded to the opposing team for all of the following playing faults, except misconduct, which may be penalized with a warning, point to the opponent, expulsion, or disqualification.

Ball Out

- A ball is out-of-bounds if it touches the ground outside the court or touches the net or any object on or outside the antennae.
- A ball is also out-of-bounds if it passes completely under the net.

Service Faults

Service Fault

- The serve does not enter the opponent's court.
- The ball touches or passes over or outside the antennae.
- A teammate touches the ball before it passes over the net.
- The server does not serve the ball within five seconds after the referee blows whistle to beckon for serve.
- A mistake is made in serving order.
- The server throws the serve, hits it with two hands, or fails to release the ball for the toss before striking it.

Foot Fault

- The server's foot touches or crosses the base (end) line before contacting the ball.
- The server's foot crosses over the imaginary extension of the sideline (stepping on this imaginary line is acceptable) at the time of contact for serve.

Ball Contact Faults

Held Ball Fault

- The ball is not played cleanly, or when a player brings the ball to a stop. *Note:* Clean handling of a ball is a matter of interpretation and varies with the skill of the players. Good referees are judged by their ability to let the players decide the outcome of a competition without putting the better (more skilled) team at a disadvantage (by how loose the weaker team is allowed to play), knowledge of the rules, and the consistency with which they judge ballhandling.

Double Contact Fault

- One player clearly touches the ball two times in a row. During a team's first contact with the ball after it has crossed the net, the ball may touch multiple parts of a player's body if there is a single attempt to play the ball. Note that a block does not count as a contact and a team is permitted three contacts after touching the ball on a block. Indeed, a player may block the ball and then immediately attack the ball (without another player having touched the ball) if the ball remains in or behind the plane of the net.

Four Hits Fault

- A team contacts the ball four times before returning it to the opponent's court. Again, a block is not counted as a hit or contact.
- On rare occasion, two players are judged to have contacted the ball simultaneously and, therefore, the team is deemed to have used only one of the three available contacts. Either player may then contact the ball if another team contact is available.

Location Faults

Positional Fault

- Any player is not in her correct position in relation to teammates when the ball is served.

Limitations for Back Line Players (Including the Libero)

- Back line players return the ball from the front zone at a level higher than the net to the opponent's court, or a back line player participates in a block.
- The libero sets the ball to a front row player using overhand finger action when any part of the libero's body touches the court on or in front of the three meter line and the front row player contacts the ball above the height of the net directing it across the net.
- The libero contacts the ball above the height of the net anywhere on the court and directs it across the net.
- The libero serves (except in U.S. college competition).

Net Faults

Contact With the Net Fault

- A player making a play touches the top of the net or the antennae in an attempt to play the ball.
- A player interferes with or disrupts the opponent's play by contacting the net below its top.

Penetration Faults

- Reaching over the net: A player crosses over the net to touch a ball that is in the opponent's court. This prohibition does not apply to blocking an opponent's third contact or any ball directed toward the net. Note that a player cannot bring back onto his side of the net a ball which has entered the plane of the net (the vertical space immediately above the net) on a team's first or second contact of the ball.
- Penetration under the net: A foot completely enters and touches the opponent's court (with no part of the foot on or above the center line).

Blocking Faults

- The ball is touched over the net and in opponent's side of the court on the outside of the antenna.
- The block interferes with the opponent's legal play completely on the opponent's side of the net.
- The opponent's serve is blocked (or hit back into the opponent's court).

Misconduct

- Unsportsmanlike conduct: Delay of game, threatening the opponent's players in a loud voice, etc.
- Rude conduct: A player acts or speaks offensively or threateningly to opponents or the referee.

References

Beal, D. (1989). "Basic Team System and Tactics" in *FIVB Coaches Manual* I. Direct Marketing and Communication SA.

    A guide edited by the FIVB (Fédération Internationale de Volleyball), written by coaches with international experience.

Döbler, H. (1985). *Kyūgi Undōgaku* (translation of *Abriß einer Theorie der Sportspiele*). Norimasa Tanigama (trans.). Fumaido Publishers.

    An essay that systematically approaches the theories behind ball sports from various perspectives.

Itagaki, Y. (1989). *Kyūgi no Senjutsu Taikei Joron (An Introduction to the Tactics of Ball Sports)*. Azusa Publishers.

    An essay that compares the theories behind strategies used in volleyball and basketball.

Japanese Volleyball Association (1995). *Tournament Rules (For Six Players)*.

Japanese Volleyball Association (1990). Volleyball Next Dynamism (unpublished materials).

    Materials commissioned from private companies by the Japanese Volleyball Association as an idea to expand the popularity of volleyball in Japan.

Nakano, T. (1989). Barēbōru ni Okeru Tanoshisa ni Kansuru Kennkyu (Research on the Enjoyment of Volleyball). Tokyo Gakugei University Thesis.

    A thesis that presents research analyzing the enjoyment of volleyball by college players.

Neville, W.J. (1990). *Coaching Volleyball Successfully*. Leisure Press.

    A book that provides knowledge about techniques and drill development necessary to volleyball coaches.

Odano, T. & Tochihori, N. (1987). *Barēbōru no Gakushu Shidou (Learning Volleyball)*. Fumaido Publishers.

    A manual that describes effective methods for teachers of volleyball in school physical education classes.

Ogan, T., et al. (1996). *Illustrated Volleyball: Skills and Coaching Guide*. Fumaido Publishers.

    A book that presents skills and strategies, as well as keys to skill development and practice drills, and explains the underlying rationale for success in volleyball.

Selinger, A. & Ackerman-Blount, J. (1993). *Serinjā no Pawā Barēbōru* (translation of Power Volleyball). Nobuji Tochihori (ed.). Tsuneo Tozawa (trans.). Baseball Magazine Co.

A book filled with the wisdom of Arie Selinger, who led the U.S. Women's volleyball team to a gold medal in the Los Angeles Olympics.

Yoshida, T. (1988). *Barēbōru Maindo (The Volleyball Mindset)*. Dōwashoin.

A manual that emphasizes the importance of the "volleyball mindset," and introduces the psychology of volleyball and some unique characteristics of the sport.

Yoshida, T. (1995). "A Practical Exam for Middle School Physical Education" in *Volleyball* (p. 157). Gakushu Kenkyu Co.

About the Authors

Bob Bertucci is the head women's volleyball coach at Lehigh University, a position he assumed in 2011. Previously, he was the head women's volleyball coach at Temple University from 1995 to 2010. He has also served in the same position at Rutgers, The State University of New Jersey, the University of Tennessee, and the U.S. Military Academy at West Point. He was named the Atlantic 10 Coach of the Year in 1997, 1999, and 2002. He was also selected as the EIVA Coach of the Year in 1988, 1990, and 1992 and the Southeastern Conference Coach of the Year in 1984. Bertucci's teams have made 12 NCAA appearances, including a trip to the Final Four in 1990, and have won 10 conference championships. During his exceptional career, he has developed and coached eight All-Americans and 46 All-Conference athletes.

In addition to his collegiate coaching, Bertucci was heavily involved on several levels with USA Volleyball, including eight years on the coaching staff of the women's national team. He coached the 1999 U.S. Women's World University Games team in Spain; the 1985 Women's World University Games team in Kobe, Japan; two U.S. Olympic Festivals; and the U.S. Women's Junior National Team. He also spent three years on the board of directors for the United States Volleyball Association.

A member of the YMCA Volleyball Hall of Fame and the Staten Island Sports Hall of Fame, Bertucci has authored more than a half dozen books and has been featured on 11 well-received instructional videos/DVDs on volleyball.

Toshiaki Yoshida is the head volleyball coach at Ageo Medics, a position he has held since 2009. Previously, he was the head coach of the Pioneer Red Wings from 2006 to 2008. He was a professor at Biwako Seikei Sport College in Japan in 2005. He served as the USA Women's national head coach from 2001 to 2004 and as assistant coach from 1998 to 2000. He also served as head coach for the Tierp (Sweden) volleyball team (1997-1998), Tokyo Gakugei University (1984-1997), and the Hitachi (Japan) volleyball team (1982-83). He is a member of the FIVB coaching commission and a review member of the *International Journal of Volleyball Research*. He is the author of the book *Inside out of Passing*, and has authored or co-authored several books published in Japan, including *Kabe wa Yabureru, Coaching for Junior Volleyball, Technique and Coaching in Volleyball*, and *Bareboru Maindo (The Volleyball Mindset)*.

Makoto Katsumoto is a professor at the University of Ibaraki in Japan, where he has also served as the head men's and women's volleyball coach since 1991. Previously, he was a coach and professor at Kwassui Women's Junior College in Japan (1984-1991). He was a member of the Japanese Suntory volleyball team from 1983 to 1984. In

1992, he received coaching accreditation from the International Volleyball Federation. He is author/co-author of two books published in Japan: *Technique and Coaching in Volleyball* and *Shintai Katsudou no Kagaku (The Science of Physical Activity)*.

Yasumi Nakanishi is an associate professor and the head women's volleyball coach at University of Tsukuba in Japan, a position he has held since 2002. From 1999 to 2001, he served as the assistant coach of the university's men's volleyball team. He was head coach of Japan's World University Games team in 2005 and 2011 and assistant coach in 2007 and 2009. Previously, he served as head volleyball coach at the Japanese Women's College of Physical Education (1994-1999), where he also worked as an assistant professor from 1993 to 1999. In 1992, he received coaching accreditation from the International Volleyball Federation. He is a co-author of *Technique and Coaching in Volleyball*, published in Japan.